AF574260

The Gators and The Seminoles:

HONOR, GUTS AND GLORY

The Gators and The Seminoles:

HONOR, GUTS AND GLORY

by

James P. Jones & Kevin M. McCarthy

First edition

Published by Maupin House, P. O. Box 90148,
Gainesville, Florida, 32607. 1-800-524-0634.

Book and cover design by Vista Graphics
Cover Photo by Media Image Photography

Library of Congress Cataloging-in-Publication Data

Jones, James Pickett.
The Gators and the Seminoles: Honor, Guts and Glory/
James P. Jones and Kevin M. McCarthy.
p. cm.
ISBN 0-929895-11-8
1. Florida Gators (Football team)—History. 2. Florida State Seminoles (Football team)—History. 3. Football—Florida—Matches. I. McCarthy, Kevin. II. Title.
GV958.U523J65 1993
796.332'63'0975979—dc20 93-26971
CIP

Printed in the United States of America

The publisher gratefully acknowledges the permission and cooperation of the trademark licensing office of Florida State University and the University of Florida Athletic Association for the use of school marks and logos.

Photo Credits

Florida State Archives: 6, 10, 11, 34, 41, 57.

FSU Sports Information: 110, 111, 113, 132.

The Gainesville Sun/Stephen Morton: 180, 181, 182.

The Tallahassee Democrat: 42, 43, 67, 73, 183.

UF Archives: 26, 29, 32, 33, 37, 38, 40, 47, 48, 50, 51, 52, 63.

UF Information Services: 71, 72, 73, 76, 78, 81, 83, 121, 136, 138, 149. Gene Bednarek: 171. Neil Burger: 141, 150, 153, 154, 157.

Walter Coker: 166, 167, 168. Bruce Fink: 146. Buddy Long: iii, 161, 162, 163, 175, 176, 177. Lee Malis: 148. Herb Press: 55, 100, 101, 102, 105, 106, 117. Marshall Prine: 120, 122, 126, 127, 129, 133. Chris Runk: 141, 150. John Woodhead: 109, 112.

UF Sports Information: 16, 91, 93, 97, 118.

UF Yearbooks: 17, 19, 22, 23, 60, 66, 68, 86, 88, 144, 172.

Dedication

This book is dedicated to Briley Proctor and Clay Cushman, two second-generation fans of these two great teams. Briley the Gator and Clay the Seminole inherited their allegiances from their parents and carry orange-and-blue and garnet-and-gold forward into the 21st century.

Table of Contents

Introduction

In the weeks before the annual UF/FSU game jokes such as the following one circulated in Gainesville and Tallahassee, with the names of the coaches changing according to the head man at each school.

> Last spring Steve Spurrier and Bobby Bowden were spending an afternoon together fishing for bass on the St. Johns River. While they were looking for just the right spot in the river, a squall suddenly came up and capsized the boat. Bowden maintained his composure and managed to pull Spurrier to safety on the shore.
>
> "Bobby," a shaken Spurrier mumbled, "please don't ever tell the Gator alumni that I can't really walk on water."
>
> "Okay," Bowden replied. "But only if you promise not to tell the Seminole alumni that I saved you."

These two coaches, whom many of their peers consider the finest, most decent men in the job, are friends most of the year, except for that one time each fall when they meet on opposite sides of the gridiron.

What they are vying for on that day are bragging rights for another year, an edge in the recruiting wars, and an easier time on the spring banquet circuit. They used to vie for the Makala Trophy given by the Exchange Club of West St. Petersburg to the winner of the match. That four-foot-long wood carving of an alligator fighting an Indian recreated the legend of the Indian warrior Makala, who once tried to rid the land of an oversupply of dangerous gators. He succeeded in doing so, but lost his life in the process. Each year his spirit returns to fight the gators. In the football rivalry sometimes the Indian side would win, and sometimes the gators would win. That trophy has long since disappeared, and no one has come up with a suitable replacement.

Readers may ask how anyone could be objective about this intrastate rivalry, especially when each writer is a rabid fan about his own school's team. Suffice it to say that we have looked over each other's writing, have examined objective newspaper reports about the games, and have made friendly corrections in the other's writing.

When we began to write this history, we had to decide the title. Would it be *The Gators and the Seminoles* or *The Seminoles and the Gators*? We finally settled on a coin flip, with the winner to determine the title and the loser to decide what order to put the authors' names. The first time we flipped the coin, it landed on its edge next to a bookcase; honest! Then we flipped again, and the winner, the smarter of the two authors, picked the title; the loser, the handsomer one, picked the order of the authors' names.

Here then is the history of one of the premier Division One football rivalries of this century. While relatively young as such rivalries go, this one is particularly intense. As the two teams completed their 35th match-up, knocking off less-intensely disliked teams and psyching themselves up for the annual grudge match, we offer their fans this brief illustrated history of a rivalry that has its roots much earlier than most people realize. Whether your favorite cheer is "Scalp 'em" or "Go Gators!" we hope that this book—if not exactly reuniting families whose divided loyalties keep them rooting for different teams that one weekend a year—may settle bets on the scores, the players, and the incidents. We dedicate this book to the hundreds of players and coaches involved in the rivalry as well as to the thousands of fans who have followed the ups and downs of two of this country's finest football teams.

James P. Jones
Department of History
Florida State University
Tallahassee, Florida 32306

Kevin M. McCarthy
Department of English
University of Florida
Gainesville, Florida 32611

Steve Spurrier (left) and Bobby Bowden (right).

COMMENTS BY STEVE SPURRIER

I have been fortunate to participate in the Florida-FSU series in very meaningful games, both as a player and as a coach.

In the mid-1960's both teams played exciting, wide open football with a strong flair for passing under Coach Ray Graves at Florida and Coach Bill Peterson at FSU. Both schools had outstanding teams during this era when the rivalry was still young. These games are still vivid in memory as some of the most important games I've played or coached.

In 1964 we played for the first time in Tallahassee and lost 16-7, also a first. FSU's win propelled them into the Gator Bowl game. We stayed home.

We trailed 17-16 with a little over two minutes to go in 1965 at Florida Field and drove for the winning score in six plays. I recall waving Charlie Casey into the end zone for a 25-yard touchdown completion, and then Allen Trammell returned a desperation pass for another score as we won 30-17. That Gator team went to the Sugar Bowl as Florida's first to ever play in a major bowl.

The 1966 game was controversial. FSU thought their receiver, Lane Fenner, had caught a touchdown pass for a last-second victory. The official ruled he didn't have possession, and we hung for a 22-19 win. We went to the Orange Bowl that season and beat a fine Georgia Tech team in Coach Bobby Dodd's last game.

As Florida's head coach, our teams have played in a pair of high-scoring games in Tallahassee, and we came out on the short end both times as FSU scored 45 in each game.

The 1991 game in Gainesville was one of the most intense games I've ever been involved in as a player or as a coach. It seemed that the game could be won or lost on any single play, and we managed to beat FSU 14-9 in a great college game.

The series has matured, and both teams now field nationally-ranked teams every year. I believe this will continue in this wonderful rivalry.

COMMENTS BY BOBBY BOWDEN

Every coach has one big pressure game, and the Florida game is mine. The Miami game may have become more important nationally in the past few years, but the Florida game definitely remains my pressure game. Our boosters and fans have to live with the result all year long more than with any other game, and they make me live with it too. So many players on both teams played with or against each other in high school and that increases the intensity. I nearly never would get fired, no matter what happened in the rest of the schedule, if I could always beat Florida. But due to Florida's great success under Steve Spurrier, this game is also a true national battle and should remain so.

My first big contact with the series came in 1964 when I was an assistant coaching wide receivers. Florida was looked up to then by FSU's coaches and players as if they were Notre Dame. The Gators were so far ahead in tradition. That game, the first in Tallahassee, with a Gator bowl bid at stake, was a huge game, and maybe the most important victory an FSU team has ever had.

The FSU-Florida series has everything all the great college rivalries have except long years of tradition and with 35 games it is getting that too., Now that the series has become more balanced it is a better series. With the possible exception of the Alabama-Auburn series, I cna't think of one with greater intensity, one that is any more challenging. Since Florida is a much larger state with a greater variety in sports and lifestyle and population, our series may never become as intense as Alabama-Auburn which is fought out in a small state where college ball in the entire scheme of things is more important. Inspite of that the intensity of Florida-Florida State seems to grow every year.

My most memorable game as head coach has to be 1977, my first win against the Gators. We won on Florida Field by 37-9. It was FSU's first overwhelming victory over Florida and I will never forget the trip back. From I-10 into Tallabassee cars lined the road and people had gotten out to cheer the team. At the Stadium a huge crowd welcomed us back. I have never experienced an out pouring of fan appreciation as great as this. It made me know how important the Florida-State game is.

Preliminaries

In order to understand more fully the cheers of each side and to do those cheers as a Gator/Seminole would, note the following illustration.

Florida Football Before 1958

The first victory of the University of Florida football team was over a Florida State football team. Honest! It happened in 1902, long before the modern-day rivalry began. The previous year, Dr. T.H. Taliaferro became president of Lake City's Florida Agricultural College, the predecessor of the University of Florida. The school might have had a team before then, but it did not play any games. When the 1901-1902 school term began, President Taliaferro assigned Dr. James M. Farr, a professor of English, to become the head coach of the football team and agreed to help out with the coaching as time permitted.

On November 21, 1901, the new football team played its first game when it met Stetson University in Jacksonville. The Florida players, decked out in Blue and White, lost the game

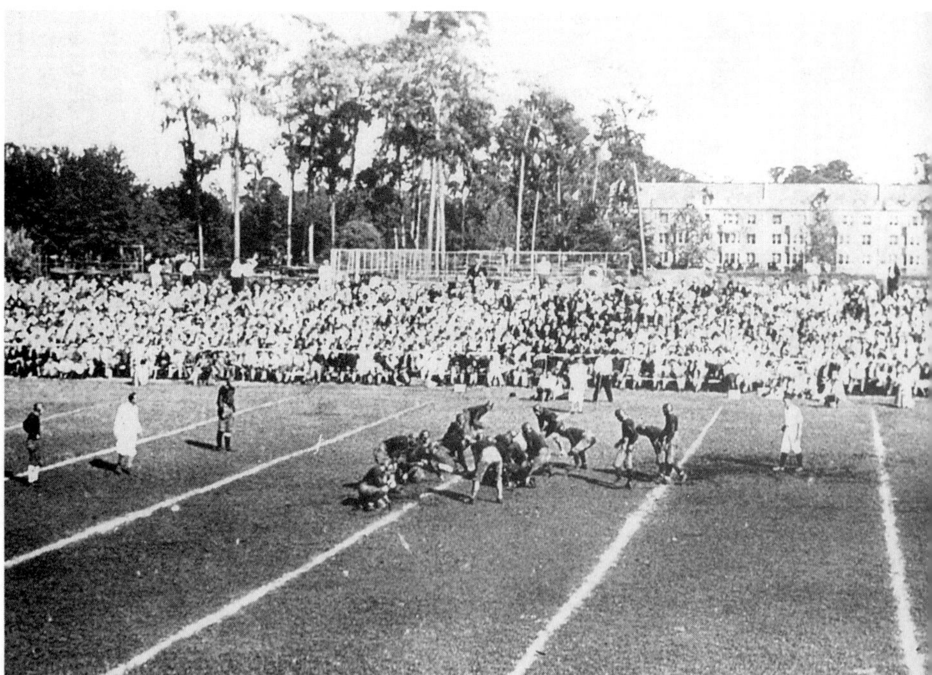

University of Florida Football.

6-0, partly because a stump in the middle of the field interfered with a drive that might have produced a touchdown. That loss was the only game the Florida team played that year and probably gave rise to the perennial Gator admonition, "Wait Until Next Year."

In the following year the Florida team had a scoreless tie and a 22-5 loss to Stetson before taking on the men (yes, men) from Florida State College in Tallahassee. In its first football victory ever Florida won 6-0; one cannot really say that victory was over Florida State University, which some Gators like to say, since the Tallahassee school did not really begin playing football until 1947. In 1903 Florida State College in Tallahassee beat Florida 12-0, after which the Florida coach quit and resumed his law practice in Jacksonville. Even then losing to the school in Tallahassee was a painful experience.

The next year a new president (Andrew Sledd) was in charge of the Lake City school, and the football team began playing out of state: Auburn, Alabama, Georgia, and Georgia Tech. The pre-Gators lost all of its games that year and, in fact, did not score a single point. The scores in the games with Alabama (29-0), Auburn (44-0), Georgia (51-0), and Georgia Tech (77-0) were embarrassing, but the team could only get better. However, when Tallahassee's Florida State College beat Florida 23-0, the local press and the alumni began grumbling about the weak team. Outscored 224-0, the local football team could only regroup and look forward to the next season.

In 1905 the Board of Control that administered higher education in Florida decided to move Florida Agricultural College to Gainesville, which happened in 1906. For its new football coach the school, renamed the University of Florida, chose Jack Forsythe, who remained for three years (1906-1908) and had a record of 14-6-2. Quarterbacking the 1907 squad was Bill Shands, who would later become a legislator, establishing a trend that other lawmakers would follow over the years; UF's Shands Hospital is named after him.

The 1908 season saw the first appearance of the alligator as team nickname. A local Gainesville merchant who wanted a pennant for the local football team was visiting a pennant maker in Virginia when the man's son suggested the alligator as the team nickname. The pennant maker took a sketch of an alligator from a library book and began the business of making alligator pennants, banners, and other kinds of paraphernalia. By that time the team was using orange and blue as team colors. Today other schools have adopted the alligator as their mascot, but Allegheny College in Pennsylvania does so more out of alliteration than out of any attachment to nearby gators, and San Francisco State University calls itself the Gators only because its original name, the Golden Gaters—after the Golden State Bridge, did not really excite much enthusiasm.

G.E. Pyle took over as head coach in 1909 and remained for five years (1909-1913). His record of 26-7-3 against the likes of Georgia Tech, Auburn, Clemson, Mercer, and South Carolina was one of the best in Gator history. His 1910 team was particularly good (6-1) in scoring 186 points and allowing only 15, 13 by Mercer and two by the Citadel. The Gators had come a long way from that 1904 team which had been outscored 224-0. 1912 saw the start of the UF-Auburn series, one that increased in intensity over the years. Pyle re-organized the athletic association and helped put Florida football on a paying basis as it attracted more and more fans. In the first game of Pyle's final season as head coach the Gators beat Florida Southern 144-0, which included 22 touchdowns, seven of which were scored by Harvey Hester—a Florida record. Auburn brought the Gators down to earth the following week by beating them 55-0.

When Pyle resigned in the spring of 1914, UF President Murphree appointed as head coach Charles J. McCoy, the coach at Sewanee Military Academy. McCoy lasted three years (1914-1916) and compiled a disappointing 9-10 record. In his final year the team did not win a game, something that would not happen again until 1946, and McCoy's contract was not renewed. Fans, who paid just a dollar for a season ticket, did more grumbling about wanting a winning team.

President Murphree then hired as head coach A.L. Busser from Wisconsin. His 1917 team did not do well; although they beat South Carolina (21-13) and Florida Southern (19-7), they lost to Tulane (52-0), Clemson (55-7), Kentucky (52-0), and Auburn (68-0). World War I and an influenza epidemic took their toll, and the Gators played only one game in 1918, a 14-2 loss to Camp Johnson. After three years (1917-1919) and a 7-8 record Busser was gone, to be replaced by William Kline (1920-1922), who had a 19-8-2 record, including a 1-0 victory over Rollins, which did not show up for the game and had to forfeit.

James A. Van Fleet, who later went on to become a four-star general and international statesman, coached for two seasons (1923-1924) and compiled a 12-3-4 record. Around that time the school enrollment was growing rapidly, and out-of-state athletes were coming to UF to play football. Also the head coach had three assistants to help in the increasingly specialized game. When Van Fleet was reassigned to another military post, H.L. Sebring became head coach and lasted three years (1925-1927), compiling a 17-11-2 record while attending the UF law school and then continuing his career and eventually becoming chief justice of the state supreme court. The 1925 Gator team was the first one to win eight games in a season.

Dr. John J. Tigert became president of the University of Florida in 1928 after President Murphree died. Charles W. Bachman then took over as head coach and lasted five years (1928-1932), during which he accumulated a 27-18-3 record. His first year (1928) was one of the greatest in the annals of Gator football. The Gators went 8-1, losing only to Tennessee 13-12, and led the nation in scoring (336 points), beat Georgia for the first time, and had its first All-American: receiver Dale Vansickle. The quarterback of that 1928 team, Clyde Crabtree, could pass with either arm and punt with either foot. That team might have had the finest athletic talent of any Gator team before or since. When Bachman left in 1932 to become head coach at Michigan State, 26-year-old D.K. (Dutch) Stanley became head coach and lasted three seasons (1933-

1935), compiling a 14-13-2 record. When pressure from supporters around the state forced him out of the job, he went on to become head of UF's Department of Physical Education and helped hire three of Florida's head coaches.

Florida had been a member of the Southern Intercollegiate Athletic Association (SIAA), which eventually broke down into several groups, including the Southern Conference. In 1932, the 13 schools south of the Appalachians reorganized themselves into the Southeastern Conference, which included Alabama, Auburn, Florida, Georgia, Georgia Tech, Kentucky, Louisiana State, Mississippi, Mississippi State, Sewanee, Tennessee, Tulane, and Vanderbilt. Sewanee, Georgia Tech, and Tulane later withdrew, and South Carolina and Arkansas recently joined up, making the SEC one of the strongest leagues in the nation.

His successors were Josh Cody (1936-1939), who compiled a disappointing 17-24-2 record; Tom Lieb (1940-1945), who had a 20-26-1 record; and Ray Wolf (1946-1949), who had a 13-24-2 record. When the 1947 Florida legislature made Florida State University coeducational, no one at the University of Florida thought too much about it. And that fall when FSU began playing intercollegiate football, no one in Gainesville could have felt threatened, especially after the FSU team lost all five of its games that fall. Little could anyone have realized how the "scalp 'em" cheer would echo through Florida Field or Doak Campbell Stadium in future years. After all, what kind of a challenge could the successor to a girls' school offer to the boys at UF?

The 1947 bill which established Florida State University from the Florida State College for Women expressly stated that "no college, school, department, or division now existing at either of said Universities shall be moved to the other University, and *all unreasonable duplications shall be avoided.*" [italics added] In hindsight, one wonders how many Gator fans would argue that the football team fielded at FSU that fall of 1947 was an "unreasonable" duplication that should have been avoided.

Universtiy of Florida campus aerial.

Floridians around the state began to take notice when the 1948 FSU team went 7-1-0. The next year the Seminoles went 8-1-0 and defeated Wofford in Tampa's Cigar Bowl. The 1950 team went 8-0, a spotless record the Gators have never attained. In the 1951 season the Seminoles began taking on major opponents like Miami and slipped to a 6-2 record. Next year's opponents like VMI, N.C. State, Mississippi Southern, and Georgia Tech resulted in a 1-8-1 record, the one victory coming over Wofford. Meanwhile across state the Gators were struggling. Coach Wolf's teams after World War II lost 13 games in a row before they finally beat N.C. State in 1947. Coach Wolf lasted for four years (1946-1949) and compiled a poor 13-24-2 record for the worst winning percentage (.351) of any Gator football coach; Gator fans used to chant "Bye, bye, Wolf," to or at Bear Wolf in his last few years as head coach of the Gators. The then-President of the University of Florida, J. Hillis Miller, had finally had enough, and Wolf was gone.

Florida officials scoured the coaching ranks to find the best person for the job and eventually hired Bob Woodruff, who had been head coach at Baylor since 1947. He would stay for ten years (1950-1959) and compile a 53-42-6 record. As Tom McEwen described it in his history of Florida Football, *The Gators*, he had one request from the board of control that regulated higher education in Florida: beat Georgia. He did that six times over the next decade, partly with a talented staff that included men that would go on to become head coaches down the road, for example Frank Broyles, Doug Dickey, Hank Foldberg, Dale Hall, John Rauch, and John Sauer. He produced respectable teams, but his poor relations with the press did not help his case.

The Woodruff years did produce some great stars, like Rick Casares, Haywood Sullivan, Jimmy Dunn, Don Fleming, Joe D'Agostino, and three All-Americans: tackle Charley LaPradd (1952), guard John Barrow (1956), and tackle Vel Heckman (1958). And then Woodruff also had the FSU problem: about whether or not to play the upstarts from Tallahassee. As Julian Derieux Clarkson pointed out in his history of the first decade of the UF/FSU series, *Let No Man Put Asunder*, momentum for the match-up began to build in the 1950s.

In 1953, when Tom Nugent became FSU's head coach, football fans around the state began agitating for a Gator-Seminole showdown. The Gators struggled in 1953 (3-5-2), 1954 (5-5), and 1955 (4-6) and might have been reluctant to chance losing to the Seminoles; they bounced back in 1956 (6-3-1) and 1957 (6-2-1), but their upstate rivals seemed to be getting stronger also. The Seminoles had an 8-3 record in 1954 plus a loss to Texas Western in the Sun Bowl; they sputtered along in 1955 (5-5), 1956 (5-4-1), and 1957 (4-6), but were playing the likes of Miami, Auburn, N.C. State, and Georgia.

In 1955 state legislators narrowly defeated a bill requiring the two teams to play each other on the football field. Officials at UF finally bowed to the inevitable and agreed to a 1958 match in Gainesville, especially after Governor Leroy Collins urged UF President J. Wayne Reitz to schedule a game between the two teams. The two athletic directors were instructed to get it done, partly to avert a legislative mandate. The Gators felt confident when they looked at their own record and then at the Seminoles' record, but they knew that a loss in that first game would be humiliating.

The Rise of the Seminoles, 1947-1958

Shortly after Florida State decided to compete in inter-collegiate football, the university's first coach, Ed Williamson, a University of Florida graduate, went to President Doak S. Campbell to ask for funds to scout Stetson, FSU's first opponent. Campbell, whose presidency of FSU's predecessor, the Florida State College for Women, had given him no experience in such matters, asked in amazement, "Do you mean you want to spy on them?" It is a long way from that meeting and that query in 1947, the year Florida State went to the grid wars, to the major college football world of 1991. For that matter, it was a long way from 1947 to 1958, the year FSU first battled the Florida Gators.

There had been a team in Tallahassee from 1902 through 1904. Florida State College, the forerunner of FSCW, which was the forerunner of FSU, played from three to six games a year. Twice in 1902 FSU battled the Florida Agricultural College of Lake city—predecessor of the Florida Gators. In 1902 the teams traded 6-0 victories. The following season FSC came out ahead 12-0. For the newly created Florida State Seminoles (they actually played their first game against Stetson without the nickname which the student body voted on before their contest against Cumberland) there was no continuity with the distant days of Florida State College. For 43 years, after the school stopped playing football, it had no football team and no involvement in intercollegiate athletics.

In 1947, when Florida State's grid history did begin, it began with an all-losing season. Ed Williamson's pick-up squad went 0-5 against small colleges from the southeast, but came remarkably close to winning three of those games. The following season the university went north to Indiana and hired Indiana Hoosier star and assistant coach Don Veller. Under

1903 Florida State College football team.

Veller's tutelage FSU immediately became a small-college juggernaut. The Tribe's first victory was 1948's first game, a 30-0 pasting of Cumberland, and that year the Garnet and Gold was 7-1. In 1949 and 1950 Veller's men recorded 9-1 and 8-0 marks respectively. In his first three years, the new coach had gone 24-1 and in 1948 played Wofford in Tampa's Cigar Bowl, defeating the Terriers 19-6.

In 1951 Florida State made a decision about the quality of its schedule. After its great success playing teams such as Stetson, Sewanee, Wofford, and Troy State, the Seminoles would turn toward major college competition. In 1951 that meant the Miami Hurricanes. Predictably, the 'Canes won 35-13, but the die was cast. FSU went 6-2 in 1951, but plummeted to 1-8-1 in 1952 with the continued elevation of the schedule. Louisville (starring Johnny Unitas), VMI, N.C. State, and Georgia Tech appeared that year.

FSU-FSCW aerial view of the campus prior to 1935.

With the major college slate firmly committed to, Florida State decided to hire a new coach, one with experience at that level. VMI's head man, the innovative Tom Nugent, who popularized the I-formation, became the university's third head coach. In Nugent's first campaign, 1953, FSU was 5-5, defeating Louisville, VMI, and North Carolina State, its first victories over the higher quality of competition.

The Seminoles began 1954 with losses to the Georgia Bulldogs and Abilene Christian before running off victories over Villanova and N.C. State. Auburn trounced the Tribe, but FSU roared back to five consecutive wins and a regular season record of 8-3. Nugent's band was invited to El Paso's Sun Bowl where a strong Texas Western (now Texas-El Paso) eleven defeated the Tallahasseeans 47-20. A significant contributor in 1954 was a young West Palm Beach halfback listed on the roster as "Buddy Reynolds." In 1993 his name on the academic scholarship and the athletic dormitory which he has generously given to his alma mater was "Burt Reynolds."

In 1954, 1955, and 1956 Florida State put up marks of 5-5, 5-4-1, and 4-6. In those three years there was a steady advance in the difficulty of the competition. Miami remained a regular, and Southeastern Conference powers Georgia, Georgia Tech, and Auburn were added. FSU failed to defeat any of that quartet, but often played them close, losing to the Bulldogs 3-0 and Auburn 13-7 in 1956. There were victories over N.C. State, Villanova, Southern Mississippi, and Virginia Tech in that three-year span.

When Florida State decided to undertake a major college schedule and began playing teams such as Miami and Georgia, many in Tallahassee had their sights fixed on one addition to their slate that evaded them: the Florida Gators. From 1951 through 1954, efforts to add UF were frustrated. In 1955 the state Board of Control (forerunner of the Board of Regents) entered the picture.

On November 18, 1955, as FSU's 5-5 season was drawing to a close, newspapers across the state carried banner headlines in what was the biggest sports story of the year: "UF-FSU FOOTBALL ORDERED!" Speaking for the board, Chairman Fred Kent, a Jacksonville attorney, demanded that the teams agree on a game in 1956. Kent's forceful words to the two university presidents, "If your athletic directors can't get together on this, get new athletic directors." The chairman added that the only reason the legislature had not passed a bill ordering the game was the board's promise to act.

The Florida State camp roundly applauded the board's action while Gators were unhappy. The UF faculty senate assailed the board's "interference in the administration of the university's intercollegiate athletic program." Another Gator charge was that Florida would lose money since FSU could not draw fans. University of Florida President J. Wayne Reitz became involved, petitioning the board for an "indefinite" suspension of the order. Reitz cited one of the most-often used excuses for postponement or delay: the difficulty in scheduling the game. To counter the scheduling excuse, Florida State athletic director Howard Danford vowed to work to arrange schedule changes to accommodate UF and said he believed a Gator-Seminole game would fill any stadium in the Sunshine State. To sweeten the pot, Danford and FSU agreed to waive a home-and-home clause until Doak Campbell Stadium could be enlarged.

In spite of all the objections, by December Fred Kent was able to report that he was "pleased and satisfied with the results of negotiations between the two schools." Paying some heed to the problems wrought by long-time fixed schedules in college football, Kent said on December 8 that the board would be content with a series opener in 1958. By year's end, with Chairman Kent and his fellow members determined that the Orange and Blue and the Garnet and Gold would face each other, it was clear that sometime in 1958 Florida State's long-anticipated dream would be realized. By 1957 the dream's ful-

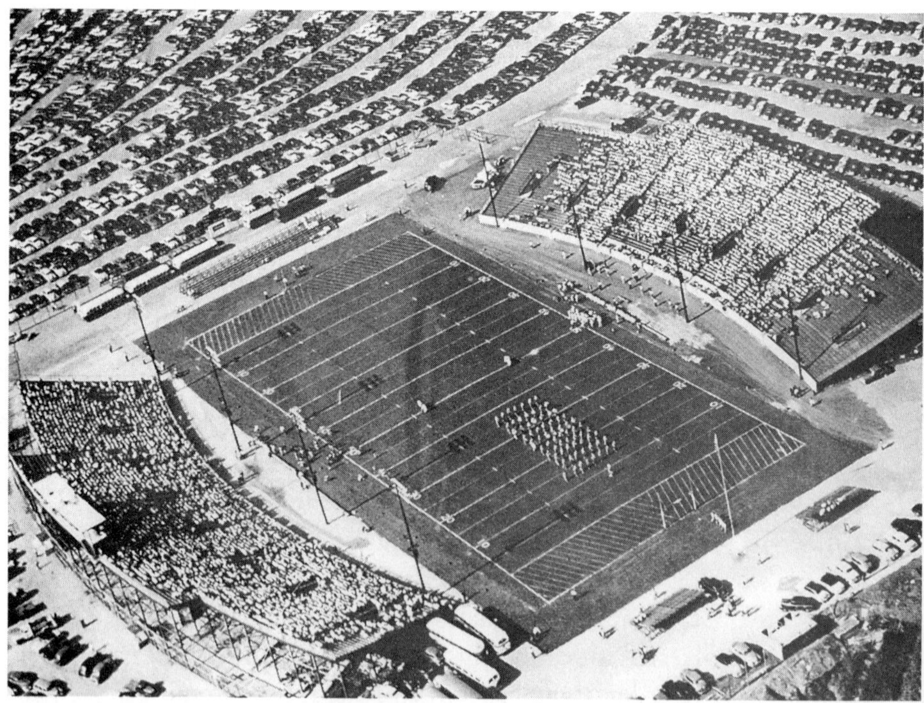

Dedication Day Game at Campbell Stadium, Oct. 28, 1950.

fillment had a specific date. On November 22, 1958, at Florida Field in Gainesville, FSU and UF would begin their gridiron rivalry.

After three 5-5 years, Tom Nugent's 1958 edition was the finest squad in his six years in Tallahassee. Vic Prinzi, a part of the FSU radio broadcast team during the Bowden era, the versatile Bobby Renn, and diminutive Tennessean Fred Pickard were the backfield keys. Leading line play were tackle John Spivey, guard Al Ulmer and end Tony Romeo.

The Seminoles began the 1958 season with decisive victories over Tennessee Tech and Furman before losing to powerful Georgia Tech 17-3. After a narrow win over the Wake Forest Deacons, FSU lost to Georgia. Standing 3-2, Nugent's men rolled to four straight victories in the games remaining before that November 22 match-up with the Gators. Virginia Tech went down 28-0, followed by Florida State's first victory over an SEC team, 10-0 over Tennessee in Knoxville. Tampa fell 43-0, and the surging Seminoles won their first game from Miami 17-6. And then the game Florida State faithful had so long anticipated. The 111th time the Garnet and Gold suited up it would be to play the Florida Gators.

1958

At Last

UF 21 - FSU 7

Did FSU offer Jimmy Dunn a one-year or a four-year scholarship? That was the question that fans talked about before, during, and after the first UF/FSU game. Seminole Coach Tom Nugent claimed he had offered Dunn a four-year scholarship, but Dunn claims it was only for one year and that he therefore chose the Gators, who clearly offered him a four-year one. The question became very relevant when Dunn was named the outstanding player of the game after helping the Gators to a 21-7 win.

The mood on both sides of the field was quite different before play began on Florida Field that afternoon, November 22, 1958. The Gators, even though they were eight-point favorites, had a mediocre 4-3-1 record going into the game. Like many of Coach Bob Woodruff's teams, they had relied on a strong defense and good kicking game and were actually ranked 12th in the nation and 7th in rushing defense after strong showings in losses to national champion LSU and third-ranked Auburn. Coach Nugent's Seminoles had a better record, 7-2, including FSU's first win over Miami and its first SEC victory, a 10-0 shutout of Tennessee. They were averaging over 22 points a game with pinpoint passing from quarterback Vic Prinzi and a 5-yard average every time Fred Pickard ran with the ball, enough to rank him 11th in the country. Fans wondered if Florida's strong defense could stop Florida State's wide-open offense.

The 43,000 fans in the stands that day had conflicting emotions. The Gator fans felt they had everything to lose and nothing to gain against their cross-state rivals. The Seminole

F.S.U. vs Florida

November 22, 1958

Price 50c

Program cover for the first game.

fans liked their newfound respectability but were not sure how they would do against a formidable rival.

The day began badly for the visiting Seminole team. Even though it was warm outside, the visitors' dressing room had the heat turned on, and no one seemed to know how to turn it off. What was turned off and could not be turned on were the lights in that dressing room, which forced some of the Seminoles to dress outside. Superstitious fans might have looked for a psychological ploy on the part of the Gators' stadium crew or even a plot by die-hard fans, but surely the Gators would not stoop that low!

UF's Dave Hudson intercepts an FSU pass intended for Bobby Renn. (1958)

The opening kickoff looked like it might be a long afternoon for the Gators. FSU's Jack Espenship received the ball at his own eight-yard line and handed it off to Bobby Renn, who raced up the sideline for the goal. The only Gator remaining between Renn and a touchdown was little Jimmy Dunn, all 142 pounds of him, the same one who had chosen the Gators over the Seminoles. Dunn managed to get by Renn's blocker and tackled the ball carrier after Renn had returned the ball 78 yards. That Espenship-to-Renn handoff-reverse was the first of countless trick plays and razzle-dazzle that FSU teams showed over the years as they went all out to beat their cross-state rivals. Five plays later FSU's Fred Pickard scored the first touchdown and the first points in this long rivalry; the score was FSU 7, UF 0. But not to worry, Gator fans! Several series later, Gator end Dave Hudson blocked Renn's punt near FSU's 20-yard-line, scooped it up, and ran in for the touchdown. That blocked punt, Renn's first in three years of kicking for FSU, may have taken much out of the sails of the Seminoles, even though the point-after-touchdown made the score only 7-7. To add to FSU's problems, Nole quarterback Prinzi was injured before the blocked punt.

Soon after that, Gator quarterback Jimmy Dunn ran for two touchdowns to make the score 21-7, which is how it ended. Joe Majors, who took Prinzi's place for the Noles, did well, completing 12 of 26 attempts for 147 yards, but his 47 minutes of offensive and defensive playing might have worn him out. Many Seminole fans that day believed that FSU would have won the game if Prinzi had remained healthy, especially when they discovered that FSU led in yards gained, 286 (97 rushing, 189 passing) to UF's 238 (219 rushing, 19 passing). The difference was probably FSU's mistakes: three fumbles and two interceptions, all of which led to Gator scores or stopped promising Seminole drives.

The Seminoles had practiced in a closed stadium the week before the game and had worked on at least one "surprise" play, something that would mark the games over the years. For their trick play in the first game of that rivalry the FSU center was to hike the ball to the deep man in a short-kick formation, and then that man would lateral it to the flanker for a quick kick. When the Seminoles lined up for it the first time that day, the Gators diagnosed it and would not allow FSU to kick.

Sports writers, who named Dunn the outstanding player of the game, praised the play of both teams. Both squads could be proud of their efforts in that first game of a long series. As Coach Nugent stated in Arthur Cobb's *Go Gators! Official History: University of Florida Football: 1889-1967* (Sunshine Publishing Co., 1967, p. 293), "Florida won the game. But the Seminoles had arrived."

UF's junior-class officers present Dunn with the game's MVP award (1958)

The Gators went on to a disappointing 6-4-1 season, including a 7-3 loss to Mississippi in the Gator Bowl. That Gator squad, which held its 11 opponents to a meager 98 points, pleased the defense-minded Coach Woodruff. The Seminoles had a 7-4 season, including a 15-6 loss to Oklahoma State in Louisville's Bluegrass Bowl. That nationally televised game for FSU would be the first of many for Seminole teams over the years. 1958 was a year of mixed blessings for the

Garnet and Gold; they beat a Southeastern Conference team (Tennessee) and Miami for the first time. And they inaugurated the Bob Crenshaw Award to honor former FSU football captain Crenshaw, who was killed that year in a plane crash; guard Al Ulmer received that first plaque, which read "To the Football Player With the Biggest Heart." Both squads were glad that initial game was over and looked forward, sort of, to resuming the series the following fall.

1959

Changes at the Top
UF 18 - FSU 8

Much of the action around the second UF-FSU game centered off the playing field. Tom Nugent was gone from the Seminoles, having gone to the University of Maryland after six years (1953-58) and a 34-28-1 record. In came Perry Moss, former Illinois quarterback with subsequent coaching at Miami and Wisconsin. Arriving in Tallahassee with a confidence that inspired the fans and press, Moss abandoned Nugent's I-formation in favor of a more wide-open offense. Players and fans had high hopes for the Moss era, but before the UF game he stunned everyone by announcing that he would be leaving FSU after only one year of coaching to become coach and general manager of the Montreal Alouettes of the Canadian pro football league.

The uncertainty over whether Moss would be staying or leaving distracted the Seminole players that year and hindered FSU's recruiting efforts with high school players. Fred Pickard, FSU's great running back, was quoted as saying that the "whole year was disheartening" because of the uncertainty about the head coaching position. One piece of good news right before the game was the announcement that Vaughn Mancha, formerly an FSU assistant who had gone on to Columbia as an assistant, would be the new FSU athletic director.

Coach Woodruff, head coach of the Gators, would also be out at the end of the season, but he did not know it at the time of the UF/FSU game. Despite the fact that the Gators' record of eight consecutive regular-season games without a loss, the longest non-losing streak for the Gators since the 1929-30 seasons, fans were upset in October 1959, when he had the team

A handshake before the game (1959).

run out the clock in the last minute to maintain a 13-13 tie with Rice rather than try for a win. Woodruff's comment that "I will gamble to win, but I'll never gamble to lose" astounded fans around the state and sealed his fate, especially when the Gators lost the next four games. They entered the FSU game with a disappointing 3-4-1 record.

The Seminoles, who had a series of injuries early in the season, were entering the game with a worse record (3-5), including losses to William and Mary (9-0) and Georgia (42-0). The injury jinx hit on Monday of game week when star runner Fred Pickard injured his leg and could not play in the big game. In another strange pre-game development, Coach Moss did not bring his team onto the field until six minutes before kickoff. Some fans may have thought he was not taking

FSU's head coach, Perry Moss, urges on his team (1959).

a chance that another injury would further deplete his troops; Moss himself said later that he wanted to eliminate the pre-game workouts in order to save all of their energy for the game itself. The truth of the matter was that the Seminoles had simply arrived too late to warm up prior to the kick-off.

The drizzle that soaked everything during the game was a fitting climax to a lackluster season for both teams. After FSU kicked off, the Gators moved 69 yards down the field to take a 6-0 lead, helped by an offside and pass interference penalty against the Seminoles. FSU fans who remembered their team's taking the same lead a year before only to have the other team win might have hoped for a similar script, but it was not to be.

The Gators held on for an 18-8 win in a game marred by fumbles and penalties on both sides. A Seminole score in the second quarter that was nullified by a holding penalty would have given them the lead and made the Gators scramble for the win, but instead the Gators were able to sputter to a victory. The most exciting moment came right after FSU scored a touchdown and a two-point conversion. With only 38 seconds remaining, the Tribe recovered its onsides kick. Quarterback Joe Majors tried three long passes, but the Gator defense prevented further scores.

The Gators' 187-pound halfback, Jack Westbrook, scored twice on good, solid rushing and was named the game's most valuable player. The Gators had 375 total yards to the Seminoles' 136, but the leading individual was FSU's Majors, who passed for 85 and ran for 18. Once again FSU's left guard, Al Ulmer, did very well, participating in 16 tackles, for which he was named the state's lineman of the week for the third time in 1959.

Later that evening the presidents of the FSU and UF student bodies had the first of a series of annual banquets meant to keep the inter-school rivalry as friendly as possible. The Exchange Club of West St. Petersburg helped the rivalry by announcing a $500 academic scholarship and trophy for the school that won the most games in all the sports played between UF and FSU.

UF went on to finish 5-4-1 and FSU had a 4-6 record. The second game of the UF/FSU series was one of the dullest, but things would change with new coaches at both schools to begin the new decade. Moss, FSU's fourth head football coach, had a disappointing year in Tallahassee, and many fans were glad to see him go. To replace Moss FSU named as its fifth head coach 39-year-old Bill Peterson, who had served as Paul Dietzel's offensive line coach at Louisiana State University since 1955, including LSU's 1958 national champion team. FSU fans were pleased when he promised "a wide-open brand of football" with lots of passing. He would be hard pressed to replace the departing Majors and Pickard; the latter set a new FSU record by rushing for 1,546 over three years and led his team in rushing for the third consecutive year. He also won the Tallahassee Quarterback Club's Sportsmanship Award.

At the end of that 1959 season Bob Woodruff resigned in the face of pressure from around the state and at the university. In ten years as Gator football coach (1950-59) he had amassed a mediocre 53-42-6 record, but Gator fans considered him too conservative. Most agreed that he had done much in establishing a strong program at UF, but that someone else was needed to take the program a notch higher. Gator fans wanted someone who would use a more wide-open offense, especially a passing game. The next coach would inherit a strong freshman team and Larry Libertore, a red-shirted quarterback who showed good promise.

1960

One Field Goal Does It UF 3 - FSU 0

The 1960s began with new coaches at both schools. FSU hired Bill Peterson, the third new head coach in three years. A native of Mansfield, Ohio, Peterson graduated from Ohio Northern and climbed from prep coaching to a job as offensive line coach of Paul Dietzel's LSU Tigers. Pete's line led the way for Heisman Trophy winner Billy Cannon and the Tigers' 1958

UF cheerleaders in the rain (1960).

national champs. In 1960, the colorful Ohioan came to Tallahassee as head coach, a position he held until 1970, when he left to coach the Rice Owls. Pete's wide-open offensive squads were annually near the top in offensive stats across the nation. His eleven-year Seminole record was 62-42-11.

In addition to gaining notice as an offensive innovator, "Coach Pete" became famous for his verbal blunders, almost as well-known as Yankee and Met manager Casey Stengel. His teams flew to games "on a four-plane engine." The most legendary Peterson gaffe came before a game when his squad gathered on the sideline for a pre-game prayer. Pete said, "Bow your heads and I'll lead you in the Lord's Prayer." He began, "Now I lay me down to sleep....'" Realizing something was wrong, he quickly turned to his starting quarterback and said, "Oh hell, Feely, you say it."

After a brief stay at Rice, Bill Peterson went on to become head coach of the NFL Houston Oilers. His stay in the NFL was short lived, and he eventually returned to Florida State to resume his friendship with Florida State President Bernie Sliger, with whom he had been close friends since the two men's days at LSU. Pete began work for the FSU Foundation, a post he still holds in 1993.

When Peterson, who had coached under Paul Dietzel at LSU, arrived to coach at FSU, he brought Dietzel's three-platoon system with him, nicknaming its parts the War Party, the Renegades, and the Chiefs. The War Party specialized in offense, the Renegades played defense, and the Chiefs played both offense and defense. Quarterback Ed Trancygier, who had come from a small school in Georgia and the University of Iowa, continued the FSU tradition of having strong quarterbacks who could pass with pinpoint accuracy for great distances.

In January 1960, UF hired Ray Graves as head coach and athletic director. Born in Knoxville, Tennessee, in 1918, he went on to receive his AB degree from the University of Tennessee in 1942. He starred as a center on his high school, college, and professional football teams and was named captain of every team he played on. He played for the Philadelphia Eagles for two years, assisted at Tennessee and for the Eagles, and then joined Coach Bobby Dodd at Georgia Tech in 1947, where he stayed for 13 years before joining the Gators. The press took a great liking to Graves, who had great one-liners as, when asked to name his starting quarterback, he responded, "Give me Libertore or give me death," followed by "In Dodd we trust"; he was referring to his option runner, Larry Libertore, and Bobby Dodd, Jr., his passer.

The first Peterson-Graves game had several ironies. FSU depended on a Gainesville player, Eddie Feely, as quarterback; UF depended on a Tallahassee player, Billy Cash, as the field goal kicker. As happened often enough over the years, former teammates and even brothers played on opposite sides. Larry Libertore of the Gators and Happy Fick of the Seminoles had played in the same backfield for Miami Edison. The UF captain, Bill Hood, faced his brother, Larry, who played for FSU. Throughout the state, then, husbands and wives and even brothers found themselves at odds about whom to root for or even to play for.

Both teams were undefeated going into the game, but they had each played only one game; in a break from the two-year tradition of playing their game toward the end of the season, they played this one on the second football Saturday of the season. The game might have been more high scoring if they had played it later in the season, at which time the Gators and the Seminoles would have gotten used to the more wide-open offense that coaches Graves and Peterson came to use. Fans expected a high-scoring contest since UF had trounced George Washington 30-7 the previous week, while FSU had beaten Richmond 28-0. The Gator quarterback, 138-pound Larry Libertore, continued to amaze spectators and sports writers, who took to calling him "The Fly" and "The Hummingbird." FSU fans expected much of halfback Bud Whitehead, who went on to win the Tallahassee Quarterback Club's Award as the team's most valuable player that year, and guard Abner Bigbie, who won the team's Bob Crenshaw Award and was the only Seminole to make the first team Florida all-state.

The game was expected to be a high-scoring, passing duel, but turned out to be a 3-0 win—with a field goal the only scoring. (In the second quarter, when Billy Cash kicked a field goal, few would have guessed that that would be the only scoring of the day.) In the fourth period FSU's Ken Kestner tried a field goal but failed. Late in the game Ed Feely hit Bud Whitehead on three long strikes, but Bobby Dodd Jr. intercepted the next pass, and the Gators ran out the clock. Writers named Gator halfback Doug Partin, who gained 57 yards in

UF's Larry Libertore (#14) passes while FSU's Tony Romeo (#80) leaps over Don Goodman (#45).

seven carries, as the game's most valuable player and the winner of the Governor Leroy Collins Trophy. FSU's quarterback, Eddie Feely, had the most total yards in the game with 88.

What almost overshadowed the game was the attempted bribe by two gamblers of Florida fullback Jon MacBeth. Offered $1,500 to shave points, he instead went to the police and enabled them to arrest the two gamblers before the game. The two men had also promised MacBeth $3,000 more if he shaved points in the Georgia game later that season and a $1,000 bonus at the end of the season if all worked out well. All he had to do was fumble or miss an occasional tackle.

The closeness of the third annual match between the two schools pointed out how equal they were becoming. The Gators had a slight edge in first downs (16 to 14) and overall yards (290 to 209), but they and their fans knew it would not be long before the Seminoles would beat the Gators to take home the Governor's Cup. It might be next year. And maybe next year would produce the offensive-type football that fans around the state expected from a Peterson-Graves match-up.

The Gators went on to their best record so far, a 9-2 season plus an exciting 13-12 victory over Baylor in the Gator Bowl. They beat nationally ranked LSU 13-10 at Baton Rouge and Georgia Tech 18-17 in Graves's famous "go for two" decision that ranks as one of the high points in his career. The Gators scored 156 points and allowed only 86. Coach Graves was named Southeastern Conference Coach of the Year and even received some votes for Coach of the Year in the Nation. The *Orlando Sentinel* named him Florida's "Man of the Year."

The Seminoles went on to a disappointing 3-6-1 season that would not at all predict Peterson's great career at FSU. Seminole fans could take pride in the fact that the FSU frosh under the direction of former Gator All-American Charlie LaPradd and led by Charlie Calhoun had a 5-0 record, including a 26-11 victory over the Gators. Those fans could also revel in a good recruiting season, including two out-of-staters: a 6'5" quarterback from Ohio, Steve Tensi, and a 6'1" end from Pennsylvania, Fred Biletnikoff.

1961

Kissing Your Sister
UF 3 - FSU 3

The feelings between Gainesvilleans and Tallahasseeans were definitely heating up as the annual match-up approached. When FSU coach Peterson flew into Gainesville in a private plane to scout the Gators the Saturday before the big game, Peterson asked the pilot to find out from the airport tower exactly what time it was. When the man in the tower asked the pilot who it was that wanted to know the time, Peterson instructed the pilot to say that it was Coach Peterson from Florida State. After a short pause the man in the tower radioed back, "In that case, tell Coach Peterson the big hand is on three and the little hand is on 12."

When Seminole quarterback Eddie Feely returned to Florida Field on September 30, 1961, he was expecting a better reception than Peterson got since he was playing before the hometown fans. Having spent his high school years playing for Gainesville High School (GHS), he had fond memories of the city. When he looked up to see the Florida line facing him, he saw tackle Dick Jones, who had played with Feely at GHS. That was typical of the UF/FSU series: former teammates playing for opposite sides. Also typical was the father-son play over the years; for example, Gator center Bruce Culpepper would be followed years later by his son.

Both teams came into the game 1-0. FSU had beaten George Washington 15-7 with some clever passing and running by quarterback Feely. The Gators had beaten Clemson 21-17 behind 161 yards gained by quarterback Libertore and three touchdowns scored by halfback Lindy Infante. Both teams came into the game confident of a win, the Gators hoping to keep their win streak alive over their intrastate rivals and the Seminoles hoping to break the jinx.

The first quarter would be a harbinger of what would happen all afternoon. When the Gators stalled on their first drive, Don Ringgold went back to punt, but a high snap threw him off stride and FSU's Roy Bickford raced in to block the punt and recovered it at the UF 17 yard-line. That led to FSU's only score, a field goal by sophomore John Harllee in the first quarter. In the second quarter the Gators drove to the Seminole 14, but Bickford intercepted a pass meant for Lindy Infante from Larry Libertore. Late in the fourth quarter Bickford intercepted a Bobby Dodd Jr. pass and took it back to the UF 28.

Although FSU failed to push the ball in each time, Bickford's efforts did not go unnoticed, including his six tackles; the sports writers named him the game's most valuable player, the first time a Seminole was so honored in the UF/FSU series and the first time a defensive player won. He was also named the state's back of the week and, at the end of the season, won the Tallahassee Quarterback Club trophy. Having arrived at FSU without a football scholarship, he showed just how far one could go with hard work and determination. He had hoped to be a quarterback for the Seminoles but agreed to Coach Peterson's request that he play defense.

Seminole war canoe.

The Seminole mascot.

The only scoring was a field goal by FSU's John Harllee and one by UF's Bill Cash. UF led in statistics: 15 first downs to FSU's 5 and 291 total yards to FSU's 108. The Gators' halfback, Lindy Infante, led all rushers with 69 yards. What stopped the Gators five times was their tendency to turn the ball over, whereas the Seminoles had only one turnover. FSU earned the tie by doing what the Gators would do many times over the years in that intrastate match: avoid costly turnovers and take advantage of the other's mistakes. The 3-3 tie meant that FSU and UF each got to keep for six months the Governor's Cup, which the Tallahassee Quarterback Club presents each year to the winner of the match.

The real battle occurred after the game, when FSU fans rushed onto the field at the end of the game and tore out the goal posts. While most of the 5,000 fans on the field merely watched the proceedings, enough of them engaged in fisticuffs to make it the worst after-game extracurricular battles the series

Assistant coach for UF, Gene Ellenson, & Coach Bill Peterson "fight" over the Governor's Cup after the 3-3 tie in Gainesville.

has had. The playing of the National Anthem by both bands did little to break up the melee. Even after two choruses of "Dixie" and the playing of both alma maters, it took the strong efforts of the policemen and highway troopers who had left the stadium to handle the traffic control to finally quell the fights.

FSU fans did not look on the tie as kissing one's sister. Instead it represented a parity with their cross-state rival from which the Seminoles could be expected to rise. Bill McGrotha of the *Tallahassee Democrat* wrote that the tie was "the greatest thing at FSU since the school went co-educational" in 1947. Seminole fans began insisting on a home-and-home continuation of the series beginning with the 1964 game. Ray Graves summed up a lot of Gators' sentiments when he said that "This day was like a death in the family" and that Florida State had won a moral victory. When asked how he felt about his first tie as a head coach, he said, "It depends on who you play. If we'd tied the Baltimore Colts, I'd be happy. But FSU...no."

FSU ended the season with a 4-5-1 record, while Florida also had a 4-5-1 record, the worst Coach Graves had at UF, despite the presence of offensive coordinator Pepper Rodgers. Many wondered if FSU would turn the tide the next year with their first victory over the Gators.

1962

"I have no friends at FSU"
UF 20 - FSU 7

Over the years the psychological ploys used by the coaches of opposing teams have attempted to bolster their own players and gain just the edge that might mean victory. The UF/FSU coaches have consistently warned their players not to mouth off before the game or boast or make dire predictions. Coaches have been known to post the written words of opposing players on their teams' lockers to let their players know what the opposing players think of them. But it wasn't written words that fired up the Seminoles the night before the big game in 1962.

While spending the night in Ocala that Friday night, the Seminoles happened to catch the Pepper Rodgers television show on an educational TV channel. The UF backfield coach was interviewing Gator quarterback Tommy Shannon. When asked about any friendships Gator players had with Seminole players, Shannon boasted, "I have no friends at FSU." That might have been true, especially after that evening, but he went on to bad-mouth FSU's recruiting efforts: "Seems to me that they get all the Florida rejects."

The next day, November 17, an angry bunch of Seminoles raced onto Florida Field, ready to prove how wrong Shannon was. Many of the 46,000 fans there that day thought that this would be the year the Seminoles finally beat the Gators; if so, they might have given part of the credit to Shannon's words. The first quarter ended in a scoreless defensive draw, but in the second quarter Seminole halfback Keith Kinderman powered his way into the end zone; the point-after made it 7-0, a score that lasted until UF quarterback Tommy Shannon hit Bruce

Starling for a score. Hall missed the point after, and the Seminoles went into the locker room at half-time with a one-point lead, the first time in the series that FSU led at half-time.

One adjustment the Seminoles had to make at half-time was a way to avoid the offside penalties assessed against them in the first half. The FSU center had been hiking the ball when the quarterback yelled "Blue Go." The Gators soon figured that out and began yelling "Blue Move" to signal their own shift, but the "Blue Move" yell and the crowd noise resulted in several offside penalties against the Seminoles.

The turning point of the game happened in the third quarter when the Gators' Hagood Clarke fielded a Charlie Calhoun punt at the Gator 37. The future defensive back for the American Football League's Buffalo Bills evaded the first Seminoles downfield, reached his wall of blockers, and raced 63 yards upfield for a score. Soon after that, Ron Stoner, who had played for the Air Force Academy, rushed over for another score. Fullback Tom Kelley went in for the two-point conversion, and that made it 20-7. FSU's Steve Tensi made a game of it with pinpoint passing to Hank Sytsma, Winfred Bailey, and Fred Biletnikoff, but in the end they were not enough and the game ended 20-7.

No melee erupted at the end of the game, partly because the schools' presidents and student leaders had warned students before the game not to have any fights and partly because a large show of force by policemen and highway patrolmen dissuaded the most rabid fans from ruining a fine game. The brash Tommy Shannon was somewhat subdued after the game as he admitted, "FSU was a good team. They hit as hard as anyone else, and it was a great traditional game. I hope it will continue to be this way."

The press did not name any MVP, although most felt that Clarke's punt return might have earned him the honor. The leading ground-gainer (55 yards) for the Gators was sophomore Larry Dupree from Macclenny, Florida. The fact that FSU held the halfback-fullback to 55 yards was a strong testament to their quick pursuit and gang tackling. Dupree went on

UF coaches and team members.

to be voted consensus All-SEC that year and would return to do even better against FSU the next year.

As UF Coach Graves chomped on his post-game victory cigar, he indicated how much that game meant to his players and his staff: "I think we will enjoy this victory as much as we did that Tech game in '60." He thought about the intensity of the play that day and mentioned an idea that would surface from time to time: "There was as much aggressive football as we've seen played on Florida Field today. Our own state football is pretty rough. In fact, that Florida state championship isn't a bad one to have." For the FSU quarterback he had great praise: "That Feely is a great little runner. He's a threat anytime. We knew he was going to roll out, we worked on it, but he did it anyway."

By the time he finished playing for the Seminoles that season, Eddie Feely had set FSU career records in passing yardage (1,711), completions (160), and total offense (2,346 yards).

His passing touchdowns (10) and percentage of completions (57%) were respectable for his three years on the varsity and would set standards that later Seminole quarterbacks would shoot for.

The Seminoles finished the season at 4-3-3, Peterson's first winning season at FSU, but a mediocre one compared to his later successes. He coached the South to victory in Miami's North-South game in post-season action and impressed enough high school seniors around the southeast to land a good recruiting class, including Kim Hammond from Melbourne, Florida.

The Gators finished 7-4, including a 17-7 win over Lambert Trophy winner and powerhouse of eastern football Penn State in the Gator Bowl. The fact that the winner of the UF/FSU series would go to a bowl four of the next five years indicated how good the teams had become, especially in defense. Meanwhile Coach Graves kept getting calls from his brother in Knoxville, Tennessee, about a young man who was excelling in baseball, basketball, and football. After the 1962 season ended, Graves decided to invite down to Gainesville the young athlete his brother had raved about, a young man by the name of Steve Spurrier.

An early Florida Gator mascot.

1963

"You've just gotta be lucky"
UF 7 - FSU 0

FSU's head football coach, Bill Peterson, summed up the feelings of many Seminole fans that afternoon when he said after the game, "Somewhere along the line, you've just gotta be lucky. And we weren't." He was referring to the game his players had just lost, 7-0, but also to the last half of the season, during which the Seminoles lost to Georgia Tech at Grant Field in Atlanta, beat North Carolina State in Tallahassee, and lost to Auburn in the Tigers' den.

If they had managed to find some luck that day, they could have used it to stop Gator fullback Larry Dupree, who rushed for 131 yards. His 31 carries broke the Gator record of 29 that Rick Casares had set in 1952. Dupree finished up his junior season with a total of 745 yards, which was second best in Gator history, behind Chuck Hunsinger's 842 yards in 1948. Facing defenses week after week that honed in on him, the 195-pound, 5'11" Dupree showed a stamina and doggedness that earned him election to the All-Southeastern Conference team his sophomore and junior years (1962-63) and would earn him All-American honors his senior year (1964).

He fondly remembers the afternoon in 1963 when the Gators went to Tuscaloosa to play Bear Bryant's Crimson Tide, led by Joe Namath and ranked third in the country. Coach Bryant had never lost in Denny Stadium in his six years as head coach, but he did that day. Dupree ran for close to 100 yards and had two long runs called back. He did much to help the Gators win one of their most impressive victories, 10-6.

The 45,000 fans who showed up at Florida Field for the UF/FSU game shivered through a game that saw lots of miscues: fumbles, interceptions, and many missed chances on both sides. UF won the battle of the turnovers, having a mere three to FSU's five, but each of them stopped a real scoring threat on both sides. Some commentators in the press thought the miscues were the result of the intense, aggressive play on both sides. In other statistics Florida led in number of first downs (19-12), yardage (255-201), and plays attempted (114-49). Everything seemed to go Florida's way. Even the end zones, which home teams sometimes split up to honor the home team at one end and the visitors at the other end, both had big blue letters spelling "Florida Gators." And because it was the Thanksgiving weekend, many students had gone home and had not bought their tickets at $1 apiece; that allowed UF to sell many of the 10,000 student tickets at the going rate of $5 apiece. 45,000 attended the game, 1,000 fewer than the stadium could hold.

While Dupree's 131 yards rushing dominated UF's statistics, Tommy Shannon added 31 yards and Alan Poe had 25. The Seminoles on the other hand had more balanced rushing

The Gator mascot on the UF campus.

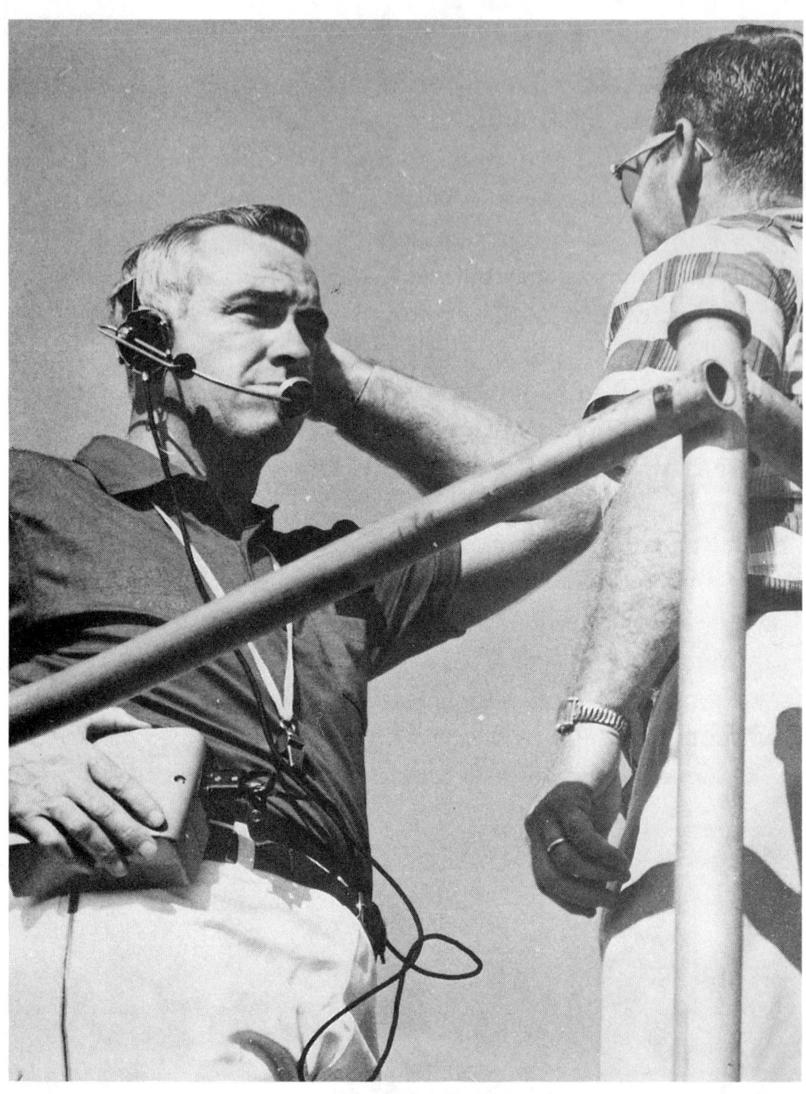

Coach Ray Graves with headset at practice.

with Larry Brinkley (38 yards), Ed Pritchett (36 yards), Dave Snyder (35 yards), and Maury Bibent (11 yards); Fred Biletnikoff caught five passes for 60 yards. The most exciting moment for FSU came with about two minutes left in the game. FSU Quarterback Steve Tensi threw a bullet pass to Biletnikoff, whom two Gators descended on and seemed to stop for a moment before he broke free and dashed 70 yards for a score, only to be called back by an official had blown the whistle when the Gators seemed to stop the speedster, at the

Gator 42-yard-line. Seminole fans would argue about that call the rest of the game. The strong wind made the teams rely on a rushing game and kept down the number of attempted passes: nine for the Gators and 13 for the Seminoles.

Dupree, still only a junior, had the game's only touchdown on one of his shortest runs, a two-yard rush only three plays into the second quarter. Jimmy Hall kicked the point after to seal the fate of the Seminoles. What had set up the touchdown was a fake field goal on fourth and three at the FSU seven-yard line. When Jimmy Hall went in to hold for Bob Lyle instead of having Ken Russell hold, Coach Peterson saw what was happening and signaled from the bench to the defense. As Peterson had guessed, Hall took the snap from center, stood up, and raced around right end to the three-yard line, enough for a first down. Two plays later fullback Dupree scored with a short run off right guard. The Florida students attending got to use their new gimmick: a rocket-firecracker that exploded over the field whenever the Gators scored.

COOL 'N' CRISP

Cooler trend prevails through tonight. High today 45, low tonight 32. Yesterday's high was 62 and the low was 30.

Tallahassee Democrat

Serving THE BIG BEND in FLORIDA Since 1905

Vol. XLIX No. 335 — Tallahassee, Florida, Sunday Morning, December 1, 1963 — Price: Daily, 5c; Sunday, 15c

Dupree Wins It For Florida 7-0

'GO, GO, GO.' YELLS FSU ROOTER SECTION AT GAME WITH UF
But the Seminoles Couldn't Pull This One Out, Losing 7-0

Democrat Staff Photo

'So Close And Yet So Far'

By BILL McGROTHA
Democrat Sports Editor

GAINESVILLE — Oh heck, just say that Larry Dupree won it.

In a crazy mixed-up kind of football game here Saturday, University of Florida pulled out a 7-0 victory over Florida State.

It was a game of many mistakes and funny bounces.

But there was nothing funny about the way fullback Dupree ran. He carried 31 times, more than any Florida back in any game ever.

And he gained more yards than any Florida back in any game ever, a whopping total of 131.

The 195-pounder from Macclenny scored the game's only touchdown on the third play of the second quarter, a 2-yard plunge that climaxed a drive of 43 yards.

THRUSTS REPULSED

Florida State repulsed thrust after thrust . . . the Gators missed a field-goal attempt after getting to the five on the heels of a fumble recovery at the FSU 23. Charley Calhoun intercepted a pass in the end zone after Florida drove to a first down on the FSU five. Calhoun recovered a fumble at the five

Caracas Defies Red Terrorists On Voting Eve

CARACAS, Venezuela (AP)—Defying death threats from Castroite terrorists, Venezuelans poured into the streets in above normal numbers Saturday—eve of a historic presidential election.

In what appeared the last gasp of a long campaign against the election, the terrorist underground fought gun battles with police, scattered tacks in the streets and burned three buses—all apparently to no avail.

Terrorists drenched the interior of another bus and its 21 passengers with gasoline, but fled before setting it on fire when they were attacked by the driver. Before fleeing, they shot the driver dead.

Above Caracas and other cities, Venezuelan air force cargo planes with powerful air-to-ground loudspeakers urged the people to vote.

The pro-Communist Armed Forces for National Liberation—FALN—which the government charges receives arms and instructions from Cuba, sought by terror to block the balloting of a successor to President Romulo Betancourt. But every indication is the voting will be held on schedule.

LEAFLETS STREWN

FALN leaflets strewn about the city warned the 1.5-million people of this capital to stay indoors until after the election or face the prospect of being shot down by snipers on rooftops. The leaflets said women and children were included in the warnings.

Four pedestrians and a policeman were wounded in gunplay in a slum district Saturday morning. Police said the pedestrians were hit by stray bullets fired in a gun fight between police and terrorist snipers.

BY DEATH THREAT

The FALN imposed its curfew by death threat as of the Friday midnight deadline that closed the campaigning of seven candidates for Betancourt's job. He is prevented by the constitution from seeking a consecutive term, but his candidate is expected to win.

During the night, terrorists slipped about the city tossing tacks into streets in an attempt to keep motorists at home. But soon afterward, street cleaners went into operation, scooping most of them up. Motorists began appearing in heavy numbers by noon — many with brooms and tree branches attached to their front bumpers to sweep away remaining tacks.

About 10,000 police, reinforced

(Continued on Page 10, Col. 5)

Jetliner Crash Fatal To 118 Being Probed

Fiery Disaster Proves Worst Yet In Canada

STE. THERESE DE BLAINVILLE, Que. (AP) — Canadian and American experts joined Saturday in a hunt for the cause of the fiery crash of a Trans-Canada DC8F jet liner that killed 118 persons.

There were no survivors of the tragedy Friday night, the worst aviation disaster in Canada's history.

The victims included Ronald Kerne, about 28, a fur buyer from Brooklyn, N.Y., and Mrs. Zoltan Hankovszky, 40, part owner of a Toronto dress factory and wife of a chef who works on a Sands Point, Long Island, estate.

The rest represented a wide range of Canadian life—including commerce, food-processing, sports, television and police work. The chief of the seven-member crew was pilot Capt. Jack D. Snider, 47, Toronto, a veteran of World War II service with the Royal Canadian Air Force.

LABOR IN RAIN

Workers labored in rain, snow and mud to recover bodies and belongings scattered over a quarter-mile section of the Laurentian countryside. Soldiers and police guarded the death zone—centered around a flooded crater containing the main wreckage — against curious sightseers and morbid souvenir hunters.

Two representatives of the U.S. Federal Aviation Agency sped in to help Canadian agents in the effort to determine why the four-engine, American-built plane—in service just 10 months—plunged to earth near this fac-

BITS

Wrong Number

TAUNTON, England (AP)—Diane Parsons will be happy soon when a new telephone directory is issued.

"I've worked it out," explained Diane. "I've said 'Sorry, wrong number' 7,000 times."

Diane is a receptionist in an optician's office. The telephone is Taunton 2541. The Taunton railway station is 2641.

"But somehow," signed Diane," the station's number got printed the same as ours —2541. About 24 times a day I pick up our phone and someone asks me about a train."

Said a spokesman for the Taunton post office, which prints the telephone directory: "We are taking extra care with the new book."

Three Missing After Sinking Of Yacht Judy

CHARLESTON, S.C. (AP)—The Coast Guard pressed its search Saturday for three persons missing after the disabled yacht Judy sank in 30-foot waves off the South Carolina coast.

Robert Stanton, 33, of Eastland, Ga., a mechanic aboard the converted Coast Guard cutter and the only survivor, was rescued by crewmen of the USS Petrel and brought to Charleston. A Navy spokesman said Stanton's condition was excellent.

Buddhist-Type Death

Girl Burns Self In War Protest

'Barest Minimum'

Johnson Backs Thrift Promise

Brick Grimes' Driving Ended For 14 Years

Brick Grimes, 1311 N. Duval St., has no driver's license and he drove a car across a

Tallahassee Democrat

Florida Frustrates FSU 7-0

GATOR HAGOOD CLARKE 33 PROVIDES PROTECTIVE COVER FOR TOM SHANNON
Putting On The Rush Is Seminole Defensive End Jim Causey

Driving Dupree Big Gator Gun

(Continued from Page 1)
Seminole bobbles and one pass. FSU was penalized 51 yards, Florida 40.

There was a crushing kind of play with about two minutes left in the game. What might have been a 70-yard touchdown play turned into a mere 12-yard gain.

Fred Biletnikoff had grabbed a short pass from Steve Tensi. Biletnikoff was stopped, but suddenly he tore loose and went the route. But the whistle had blown.

Although it was a call that might have gone either way, Biletnikoff did appear to be stopped.

FSU had three good scoring opportunities. A penetration to Florida's 18 in the first half was deterred by a Haygood Clarke interception. A drive to the Florida five was stalled by an offsides penalty and a tough defense. And a push to Florida's 27 culminated in a fumble after a pass to the 25.

As big a factor as any was Florida's ball control. The Gators got off 73 plays to just 49 for FSU. In the first half FSU had the ball for only 13 plays.

In the end Florida's offense had netted 255 yards, with 205 on the ground. FSU's 201, with 125 rushing.

• • •

Ed Pritchett, playing virtual-

The Yardstick

	FSU
First Downs	12
Rushing Yardage	125
Passing Yardage	76
Passes	7-13
Passes Intercepted by	1
Punts	4-37
Fumbles Lost	4
Yards Penalized	51

Jack Thompson grasping legs, had his toss intercept Haygood Clarke, and tha that Clarke got back to t

A 9-yard run by Dupree lowed by a piling-on penal 15, featured a Florida p the FSU 47. Dupree led the 34. Then halfback Tra threw a pass that was def by Calhoun or Winfred F or both, and Barry grabbed it for a Florida down at the 18. Dupree, runs got to the nine, and non made it a first down five.

Then Shannon tried a su throw. Calhoun intercept the end zone and raced the FSU 31, but a clipping alty put the Tribe back 10.

Soon Calhoun was p Bruce Bennett fell with th after he fielded the 40-yar at the FSU 45.

Here came the Gators.

A personal-foul penalty a 2-yard Clarke run put F at the 27. Dupree plunged 19, Clarke to the 16, and to the 10. Then Shannon

★ ★ ★ ★ ★

Seminole Statistics

FSU

If, as many would argue, the home-field advantage is worth about one touchdown to the host team, the game was a lot closer than even the low score indicated; and FSU fans continued to complain about all the games being played at Florida Field. Apart from the advantage of playing before a home crowd was the financial advantage. Even before UF and FSU split the money from the ticket sales (about $62,000 for each school), UF got to take 12.5% of the gross receipts for "expenses" plus about $10,000 for concessions sold at the game. By not playing in Tallahassee, FSU was losing more than just the home-field advantage.

Winning only once in their last four games meant the Seminoles would end with a disappointing 4-5-1 record and fail to meet the expectations of so many of their fans after their opening 24-0 win over Miami. The team had some exciting moments with the pro-type offense centered on 6'5" passer Steve Tensi, but it somehow never put all of the pieces together for a successful season. Florida finished with a respectable 6-3-1 record and the mythical state title since they had also beaten Miami earlier in the season.

Neither team would go bowling in the post-season, but FSU expanded Doak Campbell Stadium to 35,000, as stipulated by the FSU-UF contract before the game would move to Tallahassee. When some Tallahasseeans questioned the need to increase the stadium's capacity, help came from an unexpected source: Jimmy Kynes, former Gator football captain who had become Governor Bryant's assistant. Kynes insisted that the game be a home-and-home match-up in order to be preserved. Many FSU fans thought their luck would change when the Gator entered Seminole territory that next year.

1964

"The Girls' School Did It"
FSU 16 - UF 7

After six years in Gainesville, the FSU-UF game moved to Doak Campbell Stadium in Tallahassee in 1964. A campaign to increase the size of FSU's home field had pushed capacity to 43,000, and every seat was filled at the kickoff on November 21. The *Democrat*'s banner headline on game day spoke for Tallahassee and for Seminole fans everywhere: "THIS IS THE ONE!"

The Gators came into the big game at 5-2 and were ranked first nationally in pass defense. The Seminoles were 7-1-1 and fourth in the nation in total defense. The Tribe's passing combo of Steve Tensi and Fred Biletnikoff was near the top in NCAA aerial stats. On the eve of the game Biletnikoff became the first FSU gridder ever chosen first team All-American. The '64 Gators, captained by brilliant running back Larry Dupree, were determined to keep Florida's victory string alive. "Never, FSU, Never!" was stenciled on their blue helmets and "Go for Seven" was spelled out on Gator jerseys. Years later UF Coach Ray Graves admitted that the tactic "backfired" by giving added incentive to FSU.

Seminole co-captains Red Dawson and Fred Biletnikoff won the toss, and the Gators kicked off. Two plays later Florida recovered a fumble at the Tribe 19. At the 1, what Ray Graves calls the game's "key play" occurred. Middle guard Jack Shinholser drove center Bill Carr into QB Tom Shannon. Shannon recalled that the ball "hit my thigh pad and went behind me. It never touched my hands." When George D'Allessandro pounced on it and recovered at the 2, FSU had averted disaster.

Florida, though unable to score, was in control until midway through the second period. Then Steve Spurrier, who had replaced Shannon, fumbled, and Howard Ehler recovered at the Tribe 45. On their first snap Tensi fired deep to Biletnikoff, and number 25 went in untouched. While FSU threatened later in the first half, they failed to score, and halftime found the lead in FSU's hands 7-0.

The Gators' Marquis Baeszler fumbled the second-half kickoff, and alert defensive back Howard Ehler fell on the ball again, this time at the Orange and Blue 34. Driving to the 6, the Noles chose to go for three on 4th down with Les Murdock drilling the field goal. In the final quarter a Tensi to Don Floyd pass and a Wayne Giardino run pushed to the Gator 15. Once again the Florida defense stiffened, and Murdock came on to raise the margin to 13-0. Their chances for victory fading, the Orange and Blue came to life at last. Spurrier completed two short passes to Charley Casey and then a long one to Jack Harper. Running-back Harper ended the drive with a plunge to paydirt, and the Gators were only one touchdown back.

With more than nine minutes to go an assistant coach talked Coach Graves into trying an onside kick. Steve Spurrier and the Gator players were opposed, arguing that the defense could hold FSU, giving Florida ample time to move to the winning touchdown. The coach's decision held, and the bouncing ball was scooped up by the Seminoles. FSU promptly marched to a third Murdock field goal and a 16-7 lead. Spurrier's efforts to get his team back in the game were short circuited by two interceptions and a sack, and a jubilant FSU team and a predominantly Seminole crowd cheered their first series victory 16-7.

Florida State led in statistics for the game. The Tribe defense, led by linebacker Dick Hermann, middle guard Jack Shinholser, and Ehler, halted the Gator offense, limiting the Gators to just 57 yards net rushing; the Associated Press named Shinholser "Lineman of the Week" for his outstanding game. Many consider that defensive line, the so-called "Magnificent Seven," to have been the school's best defensive front wall; the

The FSU mascot applauded his team.

defensive coordinator was Don James, later the head coach of the Washington Huskies.

Tensi and his two favorite targets, Fred Biletnikoff and Don Floyd, peppered the nation's top pass defense for 190 yards and a number of key possession plays. Les Murdock's three field goals set a single-game school record and increased his season's total to nine, also a school record. FSU's offensive line was vital in the aerial game's success. Before the battle, guard Joe Avezzano (later head football coach at Oregon State) had told Peterson, "Coach, Steve [Tensi] can wear a tuxedo if he wants—nobody is going to touch him." Avezzano and his mates delivered on that promise, keeping Tensi out of the Gators' grasp all but one time.

Florida's six turnovers were a major factor as Bill Peterson's post-game interview pointed out. "We didn't make many mistakes. We took advantage of them," said the FSU head man. Pete also said that after the final gun a gracious Ray Graves shouted to him as the two left the field, "Your boys played great. Good luck in the Gator Bowl." That 20th Gator Bowl was FSU's first major post-season bowl, and they meant to make the most of it.

Florida State had taken a lot of ribbing since becoming co-ed in 1947 and beginning to play football. Ironically enough, when UF Coach Graves heard the enthusiastic cheering before, during, and after the game, he said, "I think FSU may be over-emphasizing football." One of the most widely used slurs was thrown back at those who had howled it for 17 years. On November 22, Bill McGrotha wrote proudly and with a chuckle, "The Girls' School Did It."

The Gators finished the season at 7-3 and had fullback Larry Dupree named an All-American; his 1,725 career rushing yards placed him 10th on the all-time Gator list. FSU defeated Oklahoma in the Gator Bowl, 36-19, and finished the season with a remarkable 9-1-1 record, its best record in 18 years of football. In rewriting the Gator Bowl record book that game, FSU's Tensi completed 23 of 36 pass attempts for an amazing 303 yards and five touchdowns; future Hall-of-Famer Fred Biletnikoff caught 13 passes for 192 yards and four touchdowns. That romp over the vaunted Oklahoma Sooners proved that the girls' school in Tallahassee could play football with the best of them. The Seminoles' receiver coach who would fondly remember that 1964 years later was a young man who would have much to do with FSU's later successes: Bobby Bowden.

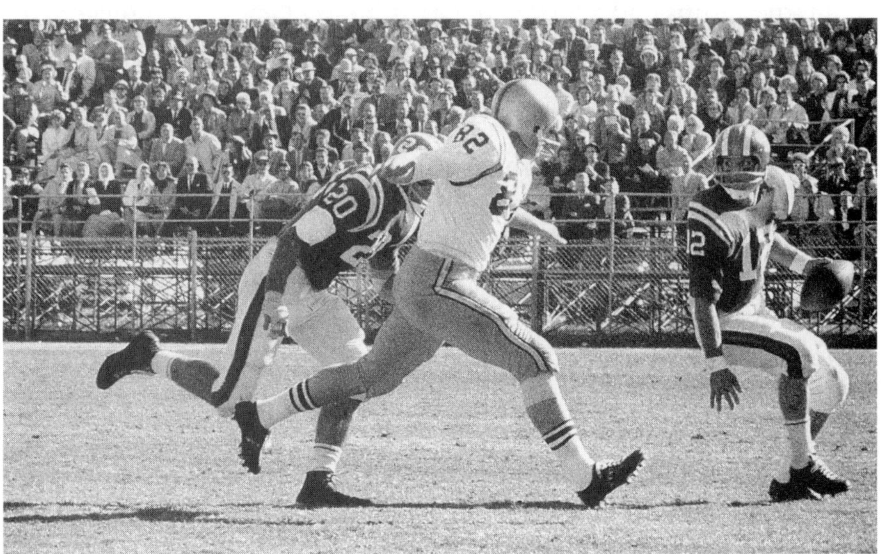

FSU's Wayne McDuffie (#82) chases UF's Tom Shannon (#12) while Jimmy Jordan (#20) blocks.

1965

"Spurrier Brings 'Em Back"
UF 30 - FSU 17

The 1965 Florida-Florida State grid battle was the last regular season game for both teams. The Gators, 6-3, were on their way to the Sugar Bowl to play Missouri and thus became the first Gator team to play in a major bowl out of the state. Florida's fine defensive end Lynn Matthews was first team All-American, while Gator wide receiver Charley Casey and defensive back Bruce Bennett joined Seminole middle guard Jack Shinholser in garnering second string All-American honors. For the Seminoles, 1965 had been a much less successful year. Bill Peterson's team stood at 4-4-1 with three losses by less than one touchdown.

Florida Field was packed with 49,513 fans as the home team, a nine-point favorite, received the opening kick. Jack Harper's runs and a Steve Spurrier-Charley Casey pass quickly moved the ball to the Garnet and Gold 20. John Feiber drove to the 7, and Marquis Baezler scored—only to have the touchdown nullified by a penalty. Baezler ran again, but fumbled, and George D'Allessandro recovered for FSU at its 13.

FSU reached the scoreboard first as the aggressive D'Allessandro, also a hero of the 1964 game, struck again. He blocked a UF punt, setting up a Pete Roberts field goal. But by halftime Steve Spurrier had taken the game in hand. On two long strikes of 52 and 37 yards, both to halfback Jack Harper, the junior quarterback moved the Orange and Blue to a 13-3 lead when the bands took the field.

When Florida State failed to move the ball following the second-half kickoff, Florida began to roll again. Led by Alan Poe's runs and Spurrier-to-Casey passes and aided by an interference call on the Noles, the Gators reached the FSU 17.

Uf cheerleaders lead the team onto the field.

When the visitors' defense halted the drive, Wayne Barfield's field goal raised the UF lead to 16-3. FSU responded at once. Phil Spooner and Joe Petko had big runs to push to the Florida 31. There on third down Nole QB Ed Pritchett fired to Max Wettstein, who caught the ball on the two-yard-line and scored to make it 16-10.

It was late in the fourth quarter before either team mustered another threat. Following a Spurrier punt, FSU began on its own 15. Pritchett and Spooner led a Garnet and Gold march that pounded to the UF 21. On fourth and four the Tribe signal-caller rolled left and threw to Jerry Jones for six yards. Roberts' p.a.t. had Seminoles cheering their 17-16 lead.

The clock showed only 2:10 left when Harper returned the kick to the Gator 39. When Spurrier left the sidelines, he turned to Coach Graves and told him not to worry. Showing the ability that would win him the Heisman Trophy a year later, number 11 took control. He threw to Casey for 10, Harper for 18, ran for 5, and fired to Casey for 13. From the Seminole 25 Spurrier rolled right and saw Casey break clear behind Tribe defenders. Waving his star receiver into the end zone, Spurrier lofted the ball into his hands for the touchdown. With 1:12 remaining the Gators were ahead 23-17.

Spurrier later recalled this play as his favorite completion of all those in his illustrious career in the Orange and Blue. "What made the play go," he remembered, "was an FSU lineman jumped offside, and I saw the referee's flag. I knew we had a free play. That's why I waved Casey into the end zone. Even if FSU intercepted, we'd still have the ball." FSU did not intercept, and Florida had the lead.

Pritchett had to throw, and the Gators were ready. At the 38-yard-line the Atlantan, who completed 18 of 34 for 193 yards and two touchdowns in the game, fired to Wetherell — only to have the defense deflect the ball into the hands of UF defender Allen Trammell, who dashed 46 yards into the end zone. Ahead with just over two minutes remaining, FSU had seen Ray Graves' men come back to win 30-17.

For a time FSU faithful had dreams of a first victory in Gainesville. Ahead 17-16, Peterson said later, "I thought a miracle was going to happen." It was not to be, and Graves had won what he later labeled "the finest victory of my coaching career." Peterson believed that "the difference was their ability

Action gets rough at the line.

The coaches share a moment together.

to make the big play." Big-play men for the Gator offense were Jack Harper, Charley Casey, Alan Poe, and especially game MVP Steve Spurrier, who accounted for 316 total yards and led the crucial drive that sealed the Gator triumph.

The Seminoles finished the season with a disappointing 4-5-1 season, while the Gators finished at 7-4, including a 20-18 loss to Missouri in the Sugar Bowl. In that bowl Gator quarterback Spurrier was named the game's most valuable player, despite the defeat, because of the records he set—most passes attempted (45), most passes completed (27), most passing yards (352), most plays (52), and most total yards gained (344). Right after the game seven Gators signed professional football contracts, continuing a tradition that saw many UF and FSU players joining the professional ranks. Coach Graves had his own contract with UF extended for five more years, which meant he would have time to try to continue beating FSU. Little did he realize that the next game in that series would be the most controversial and would be replayed many times in future years.

1966

The Most (In)Famous Game
UF 22 - FSU 19

After four years near the end of the football season, the date of the Florida State-Florida game was moved toward the beginning of the season in 1966. The Seminoles were 1-1, losing to Houston and then defeating the Miami Hurricanes 23-20. FSU had an open date before the Gators arrived in Tallahassee. Florida was riding high with three straight wins, the third over Vanderbilt the week before the FSU battle. After whipping Vandy, UF reached 10th place in the AP poll. Both offenses were ranked in the top 10, and Florida's great field leader, Steve Spurrier, was well on his way to the Heisman Trophy. Bill Peterson was well aware of Spurrier's arsenal of talents, calling him "the most dangerous player in the history of college football."

Seminole defenders would be sorely tested in trying to halt the explosive Gator offense. Spurrier, wide receiver Richard Trapp, and running back Larry Smith brought great versatility to Doak Campbell Stadium, but the small, swarming Nole defenders were ready. After the previous week's FSU victory, Miami Coach Charley Tate had said Tribe defenders, many of whom were short and undersized for major college football, scurried around the turf like field mice. Spinning off the Tate quote, Wayne Giardino, Bill Campbell, Bob Menendez, Mike Blatt, and Larry Pendleton proudly dubbed themselves the "Meeces."

In 1966 a crowd of 46,798, the largest to see FSU play in their 26-year grid history, filed into Doak Campbell. They watched as Del Williams and Bill Campbell met Bill Carr and Red Anderson for the coin toss. Florida won and elected to receive. As the Gators lined up this time—unlike 1964—there were no boastful slogans, no "Go For Seven" on their blue jerseys.

The Gators drove to a score on their opening possession as Spurrier heaved to Richard Trapp for the touchdown from the Seminole 35. While the Gator offensive stalwarts got most of the pre-game ink, FSU had its stars as well. Two sophomores from Jacksonville's Paxon High School, Gary Pajcic and Ron Sellers, were making their first appearance in the intrastate classic. Pajcic got a quick 27 yards on a QB draw and then threw to Sellers, who ran to the Gator one-yard line. When Jim Mankins rammed it in, the game was knotted at 7.

For the remainder of the first quarter and much of the second both offenses misfired, and turnovers and punts dominated. One of those turnovers gave FSU a chance, and a Pete Roberts field goal put the Noles up 10-7. With four minutes to go the Gators drove 77 yards to re-take the lead. A 19-yard Larry Smith run and Spurrier passes covered the distance. The t.d. came on the second Spurrier-Trapp six-point aerial of the game.

Florida State's Johnny Hurst fielded the second-half kick and almost went the distance, finally being halted on the Gator 27 after a 58-yard run. FSU punched it in on the ground when Jim Mankins crossed the double stripes a second time to give the Seminoles a 16-14 lead. Soon Pajcic had Florida State threatening again. At the 10, however, UF defenders led by Don Giordano threw FSU back to the 35. There Roberts missed a field goal, only to have a Gator penalty give him a second chance. This time he split the uprights. With three minutes left in the third quarter FSU had a 5-point lead, 19-14.

As the game reached the three-quarters mark, the two squads bogged down in a defensive standoff. Suddenly the Orange and Blue broke the game wide open. From his 39, Spurrier threw to Paul Ewaldsen at the FSU 41. On the following play Spurrier found Larry Smith streaking down the east sidelines, and the big back from Tampa took it the distance. When Spurrier hit Trapp for two, UF led 22-19.

Pajcic countered with a march that punched to the Florida 28 before Steve Heidt intercepted. The Gators went nowhere and punted, forcing Florida State to begin on their 14. Just under four minutes were left. Larry Green ran for nine, and Pajcic connected with Sellers for a first down. A pass to Billy Cox and a tackle-eligible throw to Jack Fenwick reached the Gator 45. On first down Pajcic fired incomplete. On second down, number 82, 6'5" reserve flanker Lane Fenner, brought in a play. The Seminoles set, and Fenner sprinted for the right edge of the north end-zone, pursued by defenders Larry Rentz and Bobby Downs. The three players leaped together, and Fenner came down with the ball. Pajcic saw his receiver grab the ball and go to the ground, certain of the t.d. and a Seminole victory. Trailing the trio, head linesman Doug Moseley started to raise his hands, but a split second later reversed himself. No touchdown—pass incomplete! Doak Campbell Stadium rocked with boos. If that play were to happen in these days of instant

The equipment box on the sidelines.

replay in the National Football League, we might have something like, "Upon further review, we have a reversal. Touchdown." But it was not to be that day.

With the clock dying, Pajcic threw to Cox on the 32, and the receiver got out of bounds. Only three ticks were left when Pete Roberts tried a tying field goal from 48 yards away. The kick fell short, and Florida had won 22-19.

The 1966 FSU-UF game produced the most famous play, the best-known controversy, in the series' history. Twenty-five years later it still stands as the best-known college football game ever played in Florida. Tallahassee *Democrat* sports editor Bill McGrotha wrote: "With the help of a touchdown that wasn't and a quarterback that was—was absolutely remarkable—Florida beat Florida State 22-19 in an incredible football game." He added words which, although true, were not about to still the anger from the Seminole camp: "Game photos indicated the official's decision was wrong, but his call was a judgement one and is final."

Fenner was sure he had scored: "I know I was in bounds until Larry Rentz hit me. If he hit me after I got the pass, it should have been a touchdown. If he hit me before, it was pass interference. I was sure I had it." Rentz, still a bit confused after the game, said: "It was right on the sidelines.... When he came down, he was out, but you couldn't tell what happened because there were so many people around."

For the next week and much of the rest of the 1966 season, the play was debated over and over. An obscure but talented wide receiver, Lane Fenner, became a household word for football fans in the state of Florida. As Bill McGrotha has said so well, "Fenner's football legacy would be one non-touchdown." Several pictures which appeared to show Fenner well in bounds appeared in newspapers and were cut out and displayed in office windows and on the desks of Seminole faithful. Doug Moseley was hanged in effigy by Florida State students.

Tribe Athletic Director Vaughn Mancha protested to the SEC supervisor of officials, saying, "We don't ask for a reversal. We don't expect a reversal because it's a judgement play. We feel

Lane Fenner catching what would have been the winning touchdown in the FSU-Florida game, but the umpire called him out.

the guy blew one and it hurts." Bill Peterson called the loss under these circumstances "a damned tragedy." He told sports writers that he did not want to blame Moseley, but added, "It's a shame." Florida head man Ray Graves sympathized with Peterson, but believed after watching the film that Moseley's call was correct. However, two decades after the game Graves mused, "My impression was that maybe we got a break." Also asked 20 years later about what had to be his most famous moment as a college official, Moseley replied at once, "I have never reconsidered because I made the right call."

Anyone looking at either the still pictures or the film must seriously question Doug Moseley's call. The official was well behind Fenner, Downs, and Rentz and in poor position to make the call. As the game came to an end, many fans came down to the sidelines, making Moseley's task more difficult. Seminoles remain convinced that Florida State was denied victory in 1966 by an atrocious call. Over the years many fair-minded Gators have admitted that the evidence that Lane Fenner was in bounds was very compelling.

The controversy obscured the fact that the 1966 battle was close and very well played. Steve Spurrier's last game in the series saw him complete 16 of 24 for 219 yards and two touchdowns. Gary Pajcic also played brilliantly, with 18 of 32 for 208 yards. Two of the series' greatest receivers, Ron Sellers and Richard Trapp, each snagged nine passes. But those performances have faded while the image of number 82, Lane Fenner going to his knees in the north end zone, remains alive. No matter what the image, the record book still reads, 1966, Florida 22, Florida State 19. Both teams finished the season with winning records: Florida State at 6-5 and Florida at 9-2, including a 27-12 win over Georgia Tech in the Orange Bowl, UF's first major bowl victory besides the Gator Bowl. Gator center, Bill Carr, who would later become athletic director at UF, was named an All-American. Steve Spurrier was named All-American for the second year in a row and won the Heisman Trophy, the award going to the best college football player in America each year.

1967

Hammond, Sellers, and Victory
FSU 21 - UF 16

When Florida and Florida State lined up in Gainesville in 1967, fans of both teams wondered how much effect the disputed 1966 game would have on motivation and outcome. FSU supporters wore badges which said, "Forget? Hell no!" The press re-ran accounts and "the" picture. Lane Fenner, the Seminoles' starting split end in '67, told the press, "I've retraced it a lot in my mind."

But this was a new game in a new season, and most coaches and players believed the previous year's controversy would have little bearing. The new season had been a successful one for both elevens. The Gators were 6-2, and FSU, after a horrible 0-2-1 start, had won six in a row. Both teams were in the AP's "others receiving votes," while the UPI had the Garnet and Gold 16th and the Orange and Blue 18th.

FSU's great combination, Kim Hammond and Ron Sellers, had kept statisticians at their adding machines. Hammond led the nation in total offense, and Sellers was number one in passes caught. Just before the game the latter made first-team All-American. For the Gators, Spurrier was gone to the NFL's San Francisco '49ers, and Larry Rentz had moved from defense to quarterback the UF offense. Richard Trapp and Larry Smith were still around, as was huge tight end Jim Yarbrough.

On game day Florida Field turned out its largest crowd ever up to that point: 62,944. Pre-game cheers and boos seemed lustier than usual. When Fenner's name was announced, it was loudly cheered and roundly booed. Then, after the Seminoles had, as usual, run onto the field before the coin toss, the Orange and Blue walked slowly through the goalposts in what came to be known as "The Big Walk-on of 1967." The Gators later explained they did it to show their disdain for the Seminoles. The home crowd leaped to its feet and roared, while Seminole fans booed from the end zones.

The Gators scored first in this one, Wayne Barfield kicking a field goal. Florida State then went ahead 7-3 after a 97-yard drive. Two long Larry Green runs were big plays, and the t.d. came on a pass from Hammond to Bill Moreman. A Florida turnover late in the initial period resulted in a second FSU score, this time on a Hammond sneak. Leading 14-3, the Noles appeared to be moving again when Hammond was injured in a face-mask foul by linebacker Tom Abdelnour. The dazed Tribe signal-caller went to the dressing room, and Gary Pajcic quarterbacked the rest of the half, which ended at 14-3.

The first second-half threat was mustered by Florida, led by Larry Rentz. The march ended when Johnny Crowe recovered a fumble for the Noles. But the Orange and Blue were not to be denied. Keyed by a brilliant catch by big Jim Yarbrough, the Gators' Tom Christian scored the six points, and Florida was down 14-9.

JF's Jim Yarbrough blocks for Tom Christian up the middle.

In the third quarter all three of the players involved in the '66 disputed play made their marks. Lane Fenner snagged a 34-yarder from Pajcic, Bobby Downs intercepted for UF, and Rentz was under center for the Gators. Early in the final stanza Florida reached the Nole 13. Mike Bugar, FSU lineman and later a Gator line-coach, put a stop to the Gator march when he threw Rentz for a loss and then recovered Trapp's fumble at the Seminole 7. Florida State lined up 93 yards away from the Gator goal. Larry Green got one yard, and FSU fans stood and roared as Kim Hammond, put back together by Don Fauls and his staff, trotted into the huddle. Hammond threw deep to Sellers, and the lanky receiver got to the Gator 41, a 51-yard gain. After Green got three yards, Hammond dropped into the pocket and heaved the ball into the north end zone. "I thought it was a duck," said Hammond. If it was a "duck," it was a long one, and Sellers soared high over Bill Gaisford, barely saw the ball in the sun, but came down with six points. Florida State led 21-9.

The Orange and Blue were not finished. A Larry Smith touchdown closed the gap to five, and, though the home team threatened again, they could not score. Florida State had its second series victory 21-16.

Post-game comments focused naturally on Hammond and Sellers. The Seminole quarterback recalled that in the first half "the lights went out" and added, "As soon as I could see clearly again, I told the doctor I wanted to go in." For his efforts Hammond was the AP back of the week. Sellers had seven catches for 153 yards. Coach Peterson summed up the feelings of many Seminoles when he said, "This win was sweeter than 1964 because it came down here."

And Lane Fenner? The Indiana split end caught two passes for 41 yards. When asked if he was glad that memories of the '66 controversy and his role in it would surely fade with the Seminoles' 1967 victory he replied, "No...I sort of like the notoriety."

That first victory at Gainesville became one of the top five "Sod Games" for the Seminoles. In a tradition begun after an

18-0 victory over Georgia in 1962, the Seminoles would take some turf home from those significant away-games that their football captains voted for. After their return to Tallahassee, the teams would bury the small plots of earth in FSU's Sod Cemetery near the entrance gate of the practice field. The marker there reads "away from home, against the crowd, and against the odds, but from the most difficult circumstances, some of the most glorious victories have been engraved." The granite headstone for each of the 60+ games has simply the date and the score.

The Gators finished the year at 6-4, while the Seminoles had a 7-2-2 season, including a 17-17 tie with Penn State in the Gator Bowl. Quarterback Kim Hammond finished fifth in the Heisman Trophy voting, the highest of any Seminole up to 1991.

Comments by T.K. Wetherell

My years at FSU as a player spanned 1963-67, and I was there also as an academic adviser the following year. For Florida State in those days, the Florida game was what football was all about. FSU players were often considered Gator rejects. When you signed a Seminole scholarship, you started hearing about being a UF reject. It made us very angry and was used to motivate us. When I arrived at FSU, there was over the training table a blank picture of the first team to defeat Florida. Florida State's ultimate goal as a football program ran through Gainesville.

For the Gator game-week there were new plays and formations, and practice was secret. You absolutely knew how important this game was for the entire program and university. You knew when it came to the Gators you were not going to leave anything in the locker room. You would play your best.

My first game against Florida was in 1964. I believe the '64 game was the first in which FSU really "knew" it could win. Florida State "came of age" that day; it was a turning point, not only in the series, but in FSU football.

The 1965 Seminole team had lost much from the victorious team of the year before, but had the seed of the powerful 1966 and '67 teams. In spite of Florida's clearly superior squad, FSU led 17-16 in the dying minutes before Spurrier's great comeback brought his team the win. I remember my most embarrassing moment of the series when, after Spurrier's toss to Casey, we were driving down field. Ed Pritchett threw to me, the ball went right through my fingers, and Trammell intercepted and scored the clinching t.d.

In the '66 game, Spurrier's senior year, only one play mattered. There is no doubt in my mind that Fenner was in bounds, way in bounds, and he had possession. After the game, we were disappointed, but, when we saw the film and realized how far Fenner was in, we got madder and madder. For the people who played in that game it will always be, "Hell No, We'll Never Forget." I still believe the FSU Media Guide should give the real score for the 1966 game and show that the Seminoles won!

Steve Spurrier on the coaches' shoulders.

1967 was my senior year. Our team with Hammond, Moreman, Larry Green, and myself — seniors — were playing our final Gator game. For Sellers, Crowe, Sumner, and the others, it all came together for us on Florida Field that day. I recall when we got off the team bus at Florida Field, Bobby Menendez, our defensive end, said, "Welcome to Florida Field. If it moves, hit it; if it don't, spit on it!" We knew we could win. Spurrier was gone, and, while they still had great players like Larry Smith and Jim Yarborough, we were sure. In spite of all the memories of Hammond and Sellers and the offense, it is the defense I remember best. They rose to the occasion and played so well when they had to. The '64 win was great, but to beat the Gators in their place was in some ways even greater. It was the end of my era at Florida State, my last game for the Seminoles, and what a way to end a career.

I have always been proud of playing in the Seminoles' first victory over UF and the first victory In Gainesville. I am also proud of playing for FSU in that era, 1964-67, the era, I believe, that put Florida State on the map and set the tone for things to come. As for playing the Florida Gators, we never had to "get up" for that game; we were from the moment we got to Tallahassee to the moment we left. The week of the Florida game was always the most spirited week of the year. The last thing seniors did as they left the practice field on the last day before the game was to tackle a dummy dressed in orange and blue.

For me, in the years since I left the playing field, the game has remained just as important. The Florida State-Florida series will always be one of the nation's best and, for me, the most important day of the season.

1968

The "Ain't No Way" Game
UF 9 - FSU 3

One of the oddest and most surprising games in the Seminole-Gator series was played in 1968. It was the second contest of the year for both squads. Florida State had beaten Maryland, and Florida, after whipping the Air Force Academy, was ranked 5th by the AP with the nation's longest streak without a loss (nine). Both teams had explosive offenses. The Tribe sent out Gary Pajcic and Ron Sellers for their senior campaigns; when Florida had the ball, the Gators would once again line up a team led by Larry Rentz, Larry Smith, and Jim Yarbrough.

Some "Lest We Forget" posters with the now very-famous shot of Lane Fenner in the end zone surfaced in 1968, but a controversy arose just prior to game day which was to take center stage this year. One of the best-known Sunshine State sports writers, the *Tallahassee Democrat*'s Bill McGrotha, had long been a strong believer in the Seminole grid program. In 1968 he wrote a column about the upcoming FSU-UF scrap that caused an instant reaction in both camps and may have affected on-the-field play. McGrotha wrote: "Florida State will win the football game. Possibly without too much sweat.... Florida has consistently out-moneyed, out-politicked, out-publicized the Seminoles. But has yet to out-coach and out-play them. If Florida somehow does pull it out, bow as graciously as you can in deference to the Gators' dedication, effort and good luck. For months I've thought about it, and it all comes to this. If it is a fairly conventional game... There ain't no way, Florida." In 1964 it had been "Never, FSU, Never!" On the other side this time it was "There ain't no way, Florida." It was the cry of the angry Gators. The impact of the *Democrat* column on the game's outcome is, of course, debatable. Several years later Coach Ray Graves said that he believed it did help motivate his gridders, while some 1968 Seminoles recall fearing that it would backfire and hurt their cause.

On a blazing September afternoon 45,256 packed Doak Campbell Stadium to see if Bill McGrotha was an accurate prophet, and some FSU fans chanted, "There ain't no way," as the teams warmed up. As they had done in 1967, the Orange and Blue walked slowly onto the field—this time to a loud chorus of boos from the predominantly Florida State crowd.

By the end of 15 minutes of play the two supposedly explosive offenses had managed no points and no serious threats. In the second period Florida went ahead on Jack Youngblood's 30-yard field goal. Deep in their own end much of the game thus far, the Seminoles had problems that continued during the second quarter. Florida's Bob Coleman sacked Gary Pajcic twice, and an FSU punt into the wind reached only the Nole 28-yard-line. With Larry Smith battering his way forward in short bursts, carrying six of seven times, Florida scored on the last of the Tampa senior's smashes, and the Gators led 9-0.

UF's Larry Smith (#33) gets closer to the goal line while FSU's Chuck Eason (#22), Ron Wallace (#83), and Harvey Zion (#71) try to stop him.

At last it seemed to be FSU's turn. Pajcic heaved for 34 to Tommy Warren, and the drive pushed to a first down on the Gator four. By fourth down the Garnet and Gold was back at the Florida five, and Coach Pete sent Grant Guthrie in to erase his team's goose egg. The field goal made the score 9-3, and that was what the board showed at halftime. After 30 minutes only 12 points and one touchdown for two of the most potentially productive offenses in the land? Surely the second half would be a different tale. But the third period was a tale of penalties, punts, and not a single additional point.

Early in the final period, following a short punt by Larry Rentz, the Tribe lined up on the UF 43. Bill Cappleman came in at quarterback and promptly hit Sellers for 15. Soon FSU reached the Florida four again with four plays to push it in. Visions of a 10-9 FSU lead leaped into the minds of the majority of those in attendance. But a tenacious Orange and Blue defense, led by Bill Dorsey, turned the McGrotha quote to an "ain't no way, FSU!" On fourth down at the three Cappleman failed to connect with Chip Glass in the end zone, and the Gators took over. The Seminoles had one other late chance, but it too failed. The final gun froze the scoreboard at Florida 9, Florida State 3.

Democrat SPORTS

A&M Trounces Allen 48-0 –Page 4C

Gators Go On Defense–Win 9-3

FSU Misses 2 Chances At a Scalp

	Page
Pete Says	3C
Play-by-Play	4C
Gleeful Graves	5C

By BILL McGROTHA
Democrat Sports Editor

Unable to score touchdowns on two occasions when it had first downs at Florida's 4-yard line, often unable to get the ball even close to Ron Sellers (or any other receivers), Florida State's football team was left disabled yesterday by tough-and-quick Gator defenders.

The score, on this hot September afternoon, was, if you would believe, 9-3.

It wasn't much of a day for quarterbacks on either side. It wasn't much of a day for offense on either side.

The Yardstick

	Florida	Fla. St.
First downs	10	8
Rushing yardage	129	62
Passing yardage	33	127
Return yardage	43	14
Passes	[illegible]	16-36-0
Punts	[illegible]	12-35
Fumbles lost	0	0
Yards penalized	67	76

UF's Mike Healey and Britt Skrivanek (#81) close in on FSU's Bill Cappleman (#41).

The two powerful offensive machines, which both scored freely in other games that season, had managed a total of only 352 yards: 190 for the Seminoles and 162 for the Gators. Pajcic, playing with a painfully sore arm, was 13 of 27 for 105 yards, and Sellers had six receptions for 50 yards. A pleased Ray Graves told a post-game press conference: "We stopped today an offense that has few peers in college football—and a receiver, Sellers, who has none." Several years later Graves remembered that his defenders, principally ace defensive back Steve Tannen, concentrated on holding Sellers up at the line of scrimmage, believing that the '67 contest had shown that stopping number 34 would halt Florida State. After the '68 game

Pete–'We Embarrassed Them Last Year And They Got Even'

Coach Peterson hailed his defense but admitted, "Our passing attack hasn't jelled yet." Gary Pajcic recalled sadly, "The whole team was just flat."

And what about Bill McGrotha and the power of the pen to influence the outcome on game day? The veteran scribe stuck to his words, saying that he believed what he had written and would do it again in the same way. In the week following the intrastate battle McGrotha wrote: "Without a surplus of football's favorable bounces it came out the way it should have come out on that day. Florida deserved to win." On Tuesday, as criticism mounted, he added, "All right...I lost the football game with that Friday column.... It got Florida all fired up and made Florida State overconfident. It provided that little edge Florida needed." Perhaps. But a "flat" Seminole offense, a sore-armed quarterback, and a very tough Gator defense were probably the more important causes for the '68 game's peculiar and unpredictable outcome.

1968, a year that head coach Ray Graves had predicted would be the "Year of the Gator" at a Tallahassee meeting before the season, turned out disappointingly for UF: 6-3-1, but two Gators did become All-Americans: fullback Larry Smith and guard Guy Dennis. The Seminoles were better at 8-3, including a 31-27 loss to LSU in the Peach Bowl. FSU's great Ron Sellers set an NCAA career pass-catching record that stood for more than 20 years and did much to make Peterson's high-powered offense so powerful.

1969

The Super Sophs—Reaves and Alvarez

UF 21 - FSU 6

Both Florida and Florida State were 2-0 as the rival squads and their followers traveled to Gainesville in 1969. The Gators had scored an amazing 106 points in defeating Houston and Mississippi State and seemed unbeatable at times. The Tribe had shut out Wichita State in a violent rainstorm and edged the Miami Hurricanes 16-14. The Orange and Blue offense, so explosive in its first two outings, was led by a sophomore aerial combination that would leave its mark on state football and on the Gator-Seminole series. John Reaves from Tampa at quarterback and Carlos Alvarez, a Cuban-born Miamian, at wide receiver had set the scoreboard alight; Reaves was fifth nationally in passing and seemed destined to rewrite the record books. The Tribe had its own strong-armed quarterback in Bill Cappleman, who was eighth in the nation in passing stats. Prior to the game Coach Ray Graves told the press that it would take four touchdowns to win. The Seminoles' Coach, Bill Peterson, had his men work in closed practices to prepare surprises for a Gator defense which had given up a surprisingly high 69 points in its first two efforts.

A full house of 63,957 filled Florida Field in spite of the rain that fell from the dark skies at kickoff. The Seminoles received and began eating up the ground. A Cappleman pass to tight end Jim Tyson and Tom Bailey's run pushed deep into Orange and Blue country. When a penalty stalled the march, Grant Guthrie came in to try a three-pointer. Cappleman fumbled the snap, and the game remained scoreless. In the second period the teams traded touchdowns. Reaves led the first drive, which ended in a ten-yard toss to Alvarez, and Florida led 7-0. FSU matched the Gator touchdown when Cappleman, barely evading a rush by Jack Youngblood, hit Don Pederson on a 22-yard score. The Tribe went for two, failed, and the Orange and Blue led 7-6 at intermission. In spite of the close score, Florida State coaches were troubled by their team's failure to protect Cappleman. Youngblood and Robert Harrell had several sacks and had hurried other efforts by the FSU quarterback.

Early in the second half the Seminoles invaded Gator territory twice, only to have a lost fumble and the stout Florida defense call a halt to their drives. It was Florida instead that got the first points of the game's final 30 minutes. Beginning at their 21, the Gators rolled. Reaves hit Tommy Durrance for 15

FSU's Bill Cappleman (#14) spots an open Arthur Munroe (#27) while UF's Jack Youngblood (#74) leaps high.

UF's Carlos Alvarez (#45) scores.

yards and Alvarez for 28. From the Tribe 30-yard-line, Reaves threw to Carlos Alvarez who was at about the one-yard line. The brilliant receiver, keeping his feet in bounds, snagged the ball with his fingertips. Alvarez's catch is one of the most spectacular made in the Florida-Florida State match-ups. The last quarter found Florida tallying one final time on a Tommy Durrance run, while the Seminoles, plagued by turnovers, saw the final gun sound with the Gators up 21-6.

John Reaves and Carlos Alvarez had been undeniably sensational in that game, but the key to the Gator triumph lay in a defense that, with some very brief lapses, was impenetrable. Bill Cappleman was sacked 11 times, and the Seminole rushing total was a minus 18 yards. Youngblood, Harrell, and company shut down an opposing offense as well as any defensive team has in the series. It is unfortunate that Harrell, a less-than-gracious victor, said after the game: "Florida State is second rate.... There's only room for one good team in the state." Bill Peterson thought he knew why the Garnet and Gold gridders had been defeated: "We lost it by making a bunch of damned

UF's John Reaves (#7) throws while FSU's Buddy Gridley (#44) defends.

Tallahassee Democrat/Sun., Dec. 3, 1989

SPORTS

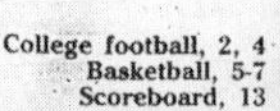

College football, 2, 4
Basketball, 5-7
Scoreboard, 13

C

DELIVERANCE

It gets a little ugly, but the Seminoles escape Gainesville 24-17

By Bill McGrotha

GAINESVILLE — Hamstrung by an aggravating bunch of penalties, and a battling opponent, Florida State's football team struggled here Saturday night.

But the Seminoles got cranked up on the record-breaking passing arm of Peter Tom Willis and whacked out a 24-17 victory over rival Florida.

Willis broke three single-season records set by Gary Huff in 1972 — for passing yardage, total yardage, total completions.

As things often seemed on the border of getting out of control, Florida State was penalized a dozen times for 134 yards, 83 in the first quarter alone. Florida, too, was flagged heavily, 12 times for 124 yards.

Just before the kickoff, Florida, wearing blue jerseys for the first time since the Kentucky game in 1979, won the coin toss and reserved its option until the second half. It was a virtually windless but chilly (61 degrees) evening.

Huey Richardson, the tough defensive end, introduced himself on the first play from scrimmage at the 20, pulling FSU tailback Dexter Carter down for a loss of 3. But on third down Peter Tom Willis passed 11 yards to Edgar Bennett at the 32.

A procedure penalty helped check FSU, and Charlie Ward punted to the Florida 30.

After Emmitt Smith struck the middle for 8, quarterback Donald Douglas got 13 on a keeper, to the FSU 49. On third down, Douglas kept it going with an 11-yard pass

stupid mistakes." But Pete could not help but pay tribute to his rivals: "They hit better than any Florida team we've ever played."

The Seminoles finished the year with a decent 6-3-1 record, while the Gators finished with a strong 9-1-1 record, including a 14-13 win over Tennessee in the Gator Bowl. Flanker Carlos Alvarez and defensive back Steve Tannen were named All-Americans that year. Super sophs Reaves and Alvarez, beginning in a crushing defeat of Houston in the opening game, 59-34, brought three years of wide-open offense to Florida, the last two under a new coach.

Before the 1969 season had begun, Coach Graves announced he would resign after that season to concentrate on being just Florida's athletic director. President Stephen O'Connell and others began looking for a head coach to replace Graves and settled on Doug Dickey, the former Gator quarterback who had gone on to coach Tennessee. Bob Woodruff, who had coached at Florida from 1950 to 1959, was then athletic director at Tennessee and hired Dickey, who had played for Woodruff at Florida. Dickey coached at Arkansas under Frank Broyles, who had coached under Woodruff for a year. After Dickey moved to Tennessee, he produced winner after winner, two SEC championships, six straight bowl invitations, and a reputation for solid, no-nonsense football.

When President O'Connell approached Dickey about the upcoming opening at Florida, Dickey said he would consider it because he and his wife were UF graduates and his mother lived in Gainesville. The fact that Florida had never won an SEC championship would be a real challenge for the new head coach. That season turned out stranger than people could have expected. The Tennessee Vols won the SEC, but then lost to the Florida Gators in the Gator Bowl, 14-13. Right after that, Dickey agreed to take the head coaching job at Florida, a decision that angered many Tennessee fans (who thought he might have had mixed feelings preparing for the Gator Bowl) and Florida fans and players (many of whom wanted Gene Ellenson, Graves' chief assistant). Dickey moved to Gainesville, but he would struggle for years to overcome that initial bad feeling he came in under and to produce a winning Gator team. He would eventually return to Tennessee as athletic director after a disappointing nine years at Florida.

1970

Huff the Magic Dragon
UF 38 - FSU 27

The fans who attended the annual battle between the two intrastate rivals included all the members of the Board of Regents, all the State Supreme Court justices, several congressmen, and six of Florida's nine university presidents state. All those officials, other than FSU's President, Stanley Marshall, and UF's President, Stephen O'Connell, remained somewhat neutral during the contest, but the 42,700 other spectators had much to cheer about as they watched a new record for points scored by both teams in the series (65) and most points by the losing team (27). The game was pretty one-sided, in favor of the Gators, until the fourth quarter.

Down 38-7 with just seven minutes left in the game, FSU's coach called on the third-string quarterback, sophomore Gary Huff, to go into the game and see if he could do something. Playing his first varsity game, Huff brought his players together in the huddle, calmly called out the play, and then completed his first pass: a 23-yard gainer to Gary Parris. On the next play Huff hit Mike Gray for a 43-yard gainer and a touchdown. Huff's two-point conversion pass to Kent Gaydos made it 38-15.

Some of the spectators who had begun leaving Doak Campbell Stadium returned to their seats, anticipating that maybe the game was not quite over. After the Gators sputtered and punted, Huff took up where he had left off. After three passes to move the ball downfield, Huff hit Barry Smith in the end zone for another touchdown. Two-and-a-half minutes remained. Could there be hope?

FSU tried an onside kick, but the Gators handled it easily.

FSU coach Peterson and UF coach Dickey.

Tensions were so high that a fight broke out emptying the two benches, and it took five minutes to restore order. The Gators stalled again and punted. In came Huff to loft another touchdown pass to Smith. The two-point conversion failed, and the game ended. Hollywood would have given "Huff the Magic Dragon" several more minutes to score a pair of touchdowns, but that was not to happen that day. What had happened was a remarkable comeback by a gutsy Seminole team.

Although the final score read 38-27 in favor of Florida, the Seminoles had found themselves a talented quarterback who would rewrite the record books at FSU before he was finished. Disdaining the run, which would have made the defense more honest but which would have eaten up valuable time, the 6'1", 185-pound Huff found his receivers with pinpoint accuracy. During the three minutes Huff played, he connected on eight of 15 passes for an amazing 230 yards. Huff's passes enabled the Seminoles to outgain the Gators, 463 yards to 402, with 418 of FSU's yards coming through the air.

The 13th meeting between the two teams almost turned out to be a lucky one for the Seminoles, but at least they showed some of the promise fans had expected early in the season. When FSU quarterbacks Frank Whigham and Tommy Warren were unable to consistently move the Seminoles downfield and when the Seminoles found themselves 31 points down in the fourth period, Coach Peterson called on Huff, and he almost pulled the victory off. That decision almost spoiled the day for Doug Dickey, coaching his first UF-FSU game.

On the Gator side, quarterback John Reaves, who had another fine outing with 13 completions in 22 passes for 244 yards and two touchdowns, praised Huff's heroics: "You see what Florida State had to do? They had to bring in a sophomore from Tampa to do something. Those Tampa boys will do it for you every time," said Reaves, another Tampa product. The 81-yard strike from Reaves to Jim Yancey in the first quarter was UF's longest scoring pass play up to that point in the school's history. Toward the end of the game Gator lineman Jack Youngblood, who had grown up near Tallahassee, stood

UF's John Reaves (#7) and Carlos Alvarez (#45).

on a wall near the FSU student side and did a very disrespectful dance wagging his rear end in the students' direction. Youngblood became the Gators' 16th All-American, not for his dancing or taunting of opposing fans, but for his great defensive play that year. He went on to star for the Los Angeles Rams in the National Football League.

That game would be the last UF-FSU match-up for Coach Peterson. At the end of the 1970 season, Rice University hired him for its head coaching position. In his 11 seasons and 115 games at FSU, Peterson had a respectable record of 62-42-11, but, more importantly, had considerably elevated the level of Seminole football. Longtime *Gainesville Sun* sports writer Jack Hairston wrote that "Peterson had as much to do with putting Florida State University football in the bigtime as anyone who ever lived" (*Gainesville Sun*, June 21, 1991: C1). Peterson would be missed in Tallahassee, not only for his great coaching but also for such "Petersonese" as "We're all in this together, and don't you remember it" and "Don't you guys think for a minute that I'm going to take this loss standing down."

To replace him FSU chose Larry Jones as its sixth head coach. The Arkansas native and LSU graduate had worked for Paul Dietzel and, more recently, at Tennessee under Bill Battle. Known for his success in developing a strong defensive unit at Tennessee, he hoped to complement the Seminoles' passing attack with a strong defense to make the team more balanced. He would go on to win the first five games of the 1971 season with that combination.

Both teams finished the 1970 season with respectable 7-4 records, but received no post-season bowls. That first year for Doug Dickey at the helm of UF football was a difficult one. With losses to Alabama, Tennessee, and Auburn with a combined score of 174 to 36 and then a 14-13 loss to Miami, the Gators struggled under their new coach. Having returned to Florida under a cloud, Dickey struggled that first year to institute his system of football; he had to cope with a new offensive line, a depleted defense, and an injured Carlos Alvarez, one of John Reaves's favorite receivers. Dickey's fortunes at UF would improve, but he would never inspire the respect and adulation that Coach Ray Graves had had.

1971

The Winless Gators vs. The Unbeaten Seminoles UF 17 - FSU 15

The Gators, winless at 0-5, were to host the Seminoles, unbeaten at 5-0 and ranked 16th in the country. Even though the game was to be played at Florida Field in front of a record crowd (65,109) and on a new artificial surface, FSU was a 14-point favorite. FSU's Gary Huff, the almost-hero of the previous year's match-up, led the nation in passing yardage and ranked third in overall offense. Coach Jones, knowing that the Gators had lost three of their five games to teams ranked in the top 20, warned his Seminoles not to be too sure of themselves: "I don't think you can afford to get confident. Not in this game." But the Seminoles had to feel confident as they looked forward to the 14th meeting between the two squads. The Gators needed to find something to change their fortunes, something to motivate them.

They found that something at 11 p.m. the previous night. Senior Tommy Durrance, the durable runner who had had so many great runs for the Gators, called the seniors together for a rap session. As those winless seniors walked down the hallway for their meeting, they began banging on the doors of all the players: seniors, juniors, sophomores, even the lowly B-team members. They all gathered on darkened Florida Field at the 50-yard line. But instead of a pep rally or a "Win one for the new coach" talk, the players let their emotions all hang out. They criticized one player for not hustling, another for missing tackles, another for not trying hard enough on pass routes. Finally defensive lineman Robert Harrell expressed what a lot of players felt: "I love this team a lot more now than I did before." The next afternoon that group of winless players whipped FSU 17-15.

FSU's James Thomas (#26) gets ready to tackle UF's Tommy Durrance (#33).

UF's Coach Dickey after the game.

Gator Coach Doug Dickey might have had something to do with lifting his players psychologically. With a variation on the half-empty-glass versus the half-full-glass he called the FSU game the opening game of the second half of the schedule. After a winless first half of the season, a victory over FSU would make the Gators undefeated at the start of the second half of the schedule.

Tensions had risen predictably in the days before the game. Florida scout Dave Fuller accused the Seminoles of delays in sending over the films that had been agreed upon in the exchange agreement. And UF officials asked former FSU quarterback Steve Tensi, who was waiting to do a radio interview with Dickey, to leave a Florida practice.

The Gators, who had relied on the strong arm of quarterback John Reaves in previous games, tried a different tactic: a running game and a tenacious defense. Reaves threw only 11 passes, completing four of them for a total of 44 yards. They rushed for a modest 152 yards, compared to 158 rushing and 198 passing for FSU, but UF's 54 rushing plays ate up the clock and kept FSU's quarterback Huff off the field. The Seminoles still managed to amass over 350 total yards compared to 196 for the Gators, but the final score is really all that mattered. And then there were the miscues. The Gators had no turnovers, compared to FSU's four fumbles and one interception.

For the Gators, fullback Mike Rich ran for one touchdown; 18 seconds later Jimmy Barr caught Arthur Munroe's fumble in the air and ran 26 yards for another UF score. Richard Franco's field goal in the fourth quarter completed the UF scoring. FSU fullback Paul Magalski ran in for a touchdown, and then Gary Huff passed to Rhett Dawson for another touchdown and a two-point conversion to make the score 17-15. In the last minutes of the game Huff moved his team down the field with crisp passing. In the most controversial play of the day Huff threw a long pass to Dawson, who caught the ball at the Gator 28, but fumbled it out of bounds when two defenders popped him. The closest official called it incomplete, much to the dismay of the Seminole fans. As happened the previous year, the clock ran out before Huff could score again in a cliff-hanger. UF captain Tommy Durance, who caught one of the four Reaves completions and ran for 60 yards, was named the game's MWP.

The Gators went on to a 4-7 season, scoring just 174 points to their opponents' 298. They also set a record for most yards allowed rushing: Alabama - 363. In the last game of the season, a 45-16 win over Miami, John Reaves broke Jim Plunkett's national career passing record with a career-total of 7,549 yards. Reaves did it by throwing 50 passes and having 33 of them caught for an amazing 348 yards; he was also helped by the infamous Gator Flop, in which the Gator defense fell down and let Miami score in order to get the ball back for Reaves to set the passing record.

FSU finished an impressive 8-4 season, including a 45-38 loss to 6th-ranked Arizona State in the first Fiesta Bowl. In that last game Huff completed 25 of 46 pass plays for 347 yards and was named the offensive MVP despite the fact that FSU lost the game. Larry Jones had had a successful first year as head football coach, even if he and his staff had gotten a very late

FSU's Paul Magalski (#31) stiff-arms a UF defender.

start in recruiting players after Bill Peterson left at the end of the previous season. The new staff and the rest of the Seminoles were definitely looking forward to the 1972 season.

Comments by John Reaves

The most memorable Florida-FSU game I played in had to be the 1971 game. The Gators had fallen on tough times with injuries, a coaching change, and a difficult schedule and entered the contest 0-5. Florida State, meanwhile, was one of the hottest teams in the country starting the season with a 5-0 record and a national ranking: of course their schedule was typically week so we felt we had a chance going into the game.

Late in the last quarter, we began a drive that was mostly on the ground and took close to 20 plays. On the first play of the second quarter, Touchdown Tommy Durrance took it in from the 1-yard line. The extra point was blocked so we led 6-0. On FSU's first play after the kick-off, Noles' running back Arthur Monroe fumbled and Florida safety Jimmy Barr picked off the fumble in mid-air and ran 26 yards for a score. We went for 2, and TD Durrance caught my pass for the 2-point play and a 14-0 lead. FSU fought back with a TD pass from Gary Huff to Rhett Dawson to cut our lead to 14-7. That was the score at halftime.

In the fourth quarter, Florida State mounted another drive and scored. They went for 2 and made it to take a 15-14 lead. With time running out, we drove to the FSU 25-yard line, where our drive stalled. Coach Dickey called on Richard Franco to attempt the 42-yarder and sent me in to hold the placement for the first time in my career. The snap was perfect, the blocking superb, and Franco split the upright's for a 17-15 win. For the seniors it was especially sweet as we finished our career 4-0 versus the Seminoles.

1972

A Long Afternoon for the Seminoles UF 42 - FSU 13

Bill McGrotha of the *Tallahassee Democrat* expressed it best when he wrote that "Florida State won the coin toss and chose not to receive. Which may have been its wisest move of a long afternoon. That way Seminoles did not get their hands on the football as much as they might have." As it was, the Seminoles turned the ball over nine of the first 11 times they had it. The Gators bobbled the ball four times but recovered it each time, in addition to taking the ball away from FSU ten times: 4 interceptions and 6 fumbles. The end result, UF 42, FSU 13, was the largest score and the most lopsided in the 15 games played thus far in the series.

The Seminoles' record up to that point (4-0), a national ranking (11th), home-field advantage for only the fifth time, and the outstanding performances of top-rated quarterback Gary Huff made them 14-point favorites over the 1-1 Gators. As always, it seemed, past records counted for nought in the annual clash. Gator senior/team captain, Fred Abbot, echoed the feelings of many players when he said, "We almost live and die to play Florida State. I couldn't even try to explain what it means to play them except it's a tremendous challenge." Superstitious FSU fans might have been somewhat chagrined when they saw the little drum that the Marching Chiefs wheeled onto the field before the game fall off its red wagon and then one of the Seminole players stumble and fall as the team ran out of the tunnel underneath the stands.

Spectators among the 43,758 fans in the stands divided family loyalties with sons or daughters attending both schools.

Governor Reuben Askew had himself attended both universities (FSU undergraduate and UF law school) and U.S. Rep. Don Fuqua's congressional district encompassed both schools.

Florida's first 35 points were the result of FSU fumbles and miscues. Gator sophomore quarterback David Bowden passed to Willie Jackson and Hollis Boardman for UF's first two touchdowns, and then sophomore Nat Moore ran for two more. In the decisive third quarter Florida scored 21 points and then put in lots of substitutes, but even they scored. Chan Gailey passed to Scott Nugent for one UF touchdown, and the defense got into the act when UF linebacker Ralph Ortega intercepted a Huff pass and ran it in for his first college touchdown. FSU quarterback Gary Huff threw to Barry Smith for a touchdown, and later Smith passed to Joe Goldsmith for a score, but it was too little too late.

The many turnovers (FSU-six fumbles lost and four passes intercepted) and penalties (UF-148 yards, FSU-75) made it one of the sloppiest games in the series. As famed sportscaster Red Barber, himself a one-time UF student and later a Tallahassee

UF's Fred Abbot (#68), Ricky Browne (#50), Clint Griffith (#78), and Mike Moore (#85) manhandle FSU's Gary Huff (#19).

resident, wrote, "The Seminoles might have handled the Gators, but they soon discovered they couldn't handle both the Gators and themselves." One example: in the second quarter, with no scores on the board, FSU held the Gators on downs and forced a field goal try to get something on the scoreboard. Dennis Aust missed the 32-yard try, but an offside penalty against the Seminoles gave the Gators a first down; on the next play Bowden hit Jackson for the first score of the game. Coach Larry Jones later said, "At halftime I thought we had made all the mistakes we possibly could make. But I was wrong. This is the worst beating I can remember."

The game set numerous records for the FSU-UF series: most points by one team (42—UF); greatest point spread between the two teams (29); most passing yards (341—FSU); and most total offense (463—FSU). Gary Huff set individual records for the series: most passing yards in one game (325); most passing attempts in one game (58); most passing completions in one game (27); most pass completions in a career (57); and most passing yardage in a career (753). He also became FSU's all-time leader in total net yardage (5,016). FSU's Barry Smith set records for most receptions in one game (10) and most yards receiving passes in one game (158). Those ten receptions helped him move into the number-one slot in the nation in that category.

The Gators finished with a 5-5-1 record, but many felt that Dickey's third year as head coach had begun to jell, that he was shaping the team in his own image, one that emphasized solid defense, an aggressive offense, and the recruitment of such skilled players as Nat Moore, Ralph Ortega, David Bowden, and Vince Kendrick. By the end of the season Moore had rushed for a school record of 845 yards on 145 carries and scored 13 touchdowns, breaking Chuck Hunsinger's single-season rushing record in 1948. Dickey had had artificial turf laid at Florida Field, instituted a weight program to beef up his players, and gathered around him a strong staff that instilled in the Gators a consistency and aggressiveness that would win its share of games in the future.

FSU's Gary Huff (#19) throws over UF's Clint Griffith (#78).

The Seminoles ended the season with a 7-4 record, including wins over Pittsburgh, Miami, Virginia Tech, and Kansas. Though a disappointing year for the FSU team as a whole, Gary Huff over his career broke several long-standing school records in touchdowns scored (54), attempted passes (839), completed passes (461), passing yards (6,725), and total offense (6,394). He continued the line of great FSU quarterbacks, a line that would become even greater in the coming years. Barry Smith, who completed the year with 69 passes for 1,243 yards, also set the school record for season touchdowns (14) and finished behind the great Ron Sellers in other categories. As a runner, Hodges Mitchell carried the ball 192 times for 944 yards for a new record.

1973

A Cake Walk Is No Fun
UF 49 - FSU 0

FSU had a poor record (0-10) going into their 16th annual cross-state match with UF and had scored only 13 touchdowns the whole season. But Seminole fans were hoping that record or the Gators' 6-4 would mean little in the annual grudge match, especially since the Gators had won their six games by a total of just 26 points. In fact, despite that winning record, UF's opponents had outscored them 171-131. In attendance were two former men associated with the football programs. UF had former coach (1923-24), four-star general James A. Van Fleet; his two-season record of 12-3-4 had the best winning percentage of any UF coach: .800. FSU had former coach (1960-70) Bill Peterson, the man who had led the Seminoles to two victories over Florida; he was between jobs, having recently been fired from the Houston Oilers. Officials dedicated the game to the memory of John Eibner, former Florida coach and director of the Gator Boosters, who had died the previous week from cancer.

FSU opened the game with an onside kick, a desperation tactic meant to surprise the Gators, but Florida recovered and proceeded to wreak havoc every which way they could. In finishing off the Seminole season at 0-11 before 62,000 fans at Florida Field, the Gators racked up 494 yards and 29 first downs against FSU's 165 yards and seven first downs, but 57 of those FSU yards and four of those first downs came on their final series against UF reserves. Freshman quarterback Billy Prescott played the whole game for FSU, another desperation move by Coach Jones, but the youngster, who had never before started a college football game and in fact had never much followed the UF-FSU rivalry since he had been more interested in the Auburn-Alabama rivalry where he grew up in Florida's

UF runner Nat Moore had broken his leg earlier in the season against Alabama, but still managed to gain 109 yards against the Seminoles.

Panhandle, could not pull off the impossible. Coach Dickey put in Robby Davis, his No. 2 quarterback, in the second quarter and played 67 Gators, but even the reserves were scoring against the injury-depleted Seminoles. The scoring was done by runners Nat Moore, James Richards, Vince Kendrick, and Larry Brinson as well as passes from Don Gaffney to Lee McGriff and Chan Gailey to Glen Sever. FSU's Hodges Mitchell closed out his Seminole career by rushing for 74 yards on 15 tries.

UF speedy tailback Nat Moore seemed to be back to his old form after recovering from a broken knee he had suffered against Alabama on October 13. In his first full-scale action since that injury seven weeks before, he carried the ball 15 times for 109 yards and scored twice in the 49-0 rout of the Seminoles, the worst defeat FSU had ever suffered. For that the 5'10", 175-pound senior was named the Associated Press Southeastern Back of the Week. Coach Dickey had called him "the most dangerous back I have ever coached" before the season began, and fans were eagerly looking forward to his recovery.

One of the strangest parts of the afternoon in Gainesville that day was the noise, or lack of same. Instead of a boisterous throng or a bevy of boo-birds, both sides were eerily silent in the stands. Even at the end of the game, when previous matches had occasionally had fistfights or jeering on each side, the players met in the middle of the field to offer congratulations or sympathy and then filed out together through the single gate leading to the dressing rooms.

While Florida players enjoyed beating their cross-state rivals, they did not want a cake walk; instead they wanted a strong rival equal to the task. UF defensive tackle David Hitchcock expressed the feelings of many when he said, "I really feel sorry for Florida State." The following Wednesday the *Tallahassee Democrat* entreated the local university to "Strengthen FSU Football Or Drop Out of the Game" since "most students don't seem to care, the alumni don't seem to care, not many fans seem to care, and there is little outward indication that the coaching staff is greatly upset."

UF Coach Doug Dickey.

After the game, FSU's worst defeat in the school's 26-year football history, Coach Larry Jones admitted that he had had some pressure to resign, "but not from anybody important." FSU president Dr. Stanley Marshall continued to support Jones, but many fans were calling for a new head coach. That 0-11 season dropped Jones's three-year record at FSU to 15-19 and certainly hurt the recruitment of the state's top players. *Tampa Tribune* assistant sports editor Jim Selman called that FSU team a "fundamentally unsound" one and "the worst college football team I have seen in 15 years of reporting the game," In the end Jones decided to resign, to be replaced by Darrell Mudra.

The easy victory gave the Gators a sixth straight victory over FSU, a fifth straight victory that season and a 7-4 record before losing to 15th-ranked Miami of Ohio, 16-7, in a freezing night at Florida Field in the Tangerine Bowl. In the middle of the season with injuries sidelining Nat Moore, Vince Kendrick, and Glenn Sever and four straight losses to Mississippi State, LSU, Alabama, and Mississippi, many fans had called for Dickey's resignation, but he hung in there and began doing the impossible, like beating Auburn at Cliff Hare Stadium (later renamed Jordan-Hare Stadium) for the first time ever, to be followed by victories over Georgia, Kentucky, and Miami. For the first time in its 67 years of football the Gators had won their final five games of the regular season and accomplished the most remarkable football turnaround by a Gator football team. Dickey, with a 4-0 record against FSU, finally seemed to be on the right path to an SEC championship, but FSU had to start over again to build a winning team with a new coach and a new attitude.

1974

"Our time will come" —But Not Yet UF 24 - FSU 14

In its new head coach, Darrell Mudra, FSU had a highly successful man who had turned around five losing teams into winners, something that FSU needed at that point. His 15 years of college coaching had produced a splendid record: 106-32-2. He took Adams State, which had been 1-9 the previous year, and led it to records of 8-1, 7-0-1, 8-2, and 9-1. He took North Dakota State, which had an 0-10 record, and led it to 3-5, 10-1, and 11-0 records, including a national title. He went on to the Montreal Alouettes, the University of Arizona, and Western Illinois with similar success stories. FSU definitely needed him.

And even though FSU was once again coming into its annual game with Florida with a winless record (0-5), the team had showed an aggressiveness, a fire missing in previous years. Florida at 4-1 and ranked 12th in the country had beaten California, Maryland, Mississippi State, and LSU, but was coming off a disheartening loss to Vanderbilt the previous week. The UF-FSU match this year was the 17th of the series and promised to be a tougher fight than the previous year's 49-0 shutout by the Gators.

The largest crowd (42,541) ever to see a night game at Campbell Stadium, the first night game of the UF-FSU series, saw a well-fought contest that was not decided until a 14-point fourth quarter. True, the Gators beat the Seminoles 24-14 for the 14th time and the 8th straight year, but the Gators had a new-found respect for their counterparts across the line of scrimmage. Both teams had new offenses: FSU with its veer-T and Florida with its wishbone. For quarterbacks FSU had junior-college transfer Ron Coppess, while Florida would alternate junior Don Gaffney and sophomore Jimmy Fisher.

In the end while Florida had more total yards than Florida State (469-353), the big difference was the fine play of Gator quarterback Don Gaffney. The Gaffney of 1973, who had done so much to inspire his team and had made crucial passes and runs, had been somewhat dormant throughout the first part of the 1974 season, but that night in Tallahassee he came alive. It was he in fact who checked off at the line of scrimmage and called the play that led to the winning touchdown. The situation was made for a do-or-die decision.

Florida was leading 10-7 and had a third-and-one situation on its own 37 early in the fourth quarter. The game's momentum had clearly shifted to FSU in the third quarter, and their offense was itching to get into the game to try for the go-ahead score. In the huddle Gaffney called for a handoff to Robert Morgan, a play that had not worked well that game, but the Gators needed only one yard for a first down. When Gaffney brought his team up to the line of scrimmage and noticed that the Seminole defenders were bunching up at the line, expecting a run, the Jacksonville junior called out, "20-Pass, go on two." With only two seconds left on the clock, Gaffney took the snap, faked a handoff to Morgan, dropped back, and threw the ball to tight end Alvis Darby, who caught it ten steps behind a defender. Gator fans gasped as Darby, nursing a sprained wrist and a bandaged right hand, bobbled the ball before hauling it in and racing 63 yards for the score that broke the game wide open. Coach Dickey later praised Gaffney: "It was a gutsy call, and he did it perfectly."

UF's Jimmy DuBose and Tony Green ran for touchdowns, David Posey kicked a field goal, and Gaffney threw to Darby for the final score. For FSU Coppess ran for a touchdown, and Jimmy Black threw to Mike Shumann for another.

Even though UF extended its series record to 14-2-1 with that seventh victory in a row over FSU, the Gators developed a

UF linebacker Ralph Ortega said that this year's Seminoles have "improved 110 percent. That quarterback Jimmy Black played one hell of a game."

great deal of respect for the Seminoles. Gator defensive back Wayne Fields said it best: "I've got to say this for Florida State. They are the most fired-up team we have ever played. That's the most guts I've ever seen. It's a helluva thing to have that kind of attitude and that kind of spirit when you are 0-18. They're just victims of circumstances." Coach Mudra had brought a new respect to the team and a new attitude. The intense physical conditioning he insisted on for his players resulted in fewer injuries than in the past. Mudra's statement, "Our time will come," would not come to pass when he was at FSU.

The Gators finished the season with a 13-10 loss to Nebraska in the Sugar Bowl and finished with an 8-4 record. Doug Dickey's fifth Gator team produced two All-Americans that year: guard Burton Lawless and linebacker Ralph Ortega. Lee McGriff, whom Dickey called "the best pass-catcher I have coached," led the Southeastern Conference in pass receptions for the second year; senior McGriff would be missed, but the great Wes Chandler was waiting in the wings to take his place. The Seminoles finished their season with a disappointing 1-10 record, but Coach Mudra had high hopes for the next year, even though he had to replace ten seniors, including tight-end Joe Goldsmith and linebacker Bert Cooper. Seminole fans had, for the most part, stuck with the team during that trying year; their support enabled the athletic staff to plan to spend some $1 million to improve facilities.

1975

Du Did It
UF 34 - FSU 8

UF and FSU entered their 18th meeting with opposite records: 4-1 for the 12th-ranked Gators and 1-4 for the Seminoles. The Gator wishbone attack was ranked first in the nation in total offense with 442.2 yards per game, and senior fullback Jimmy DuBose, who had rushed for 65 times and gained 561 yards up to that point, was averaging an amazing 8.3 yards per carry. The Seminole defense was particularly strong that year, leading the nation in pass defense and allowing only four completions in nine attempts and only 50 yards a game. The alumni were pressuring Coach Mudra to do better; some of them had bumper stickers reading "Fire Mudra. For Pete's Sake," referring to former coach Bill Peterson, the last FSU coach who had beaten the Gators (1967).

In those days the Florida game was the most important one to Seminole fans. Beating the Gators made the whole season, despite what their own record might be. Florida had so many important games, whether Georgia, Auburn, Alabama, or whatever team stood in their way for the elusive SEC championship, that they got up for the FSU game only during the week leading up to the match. In Tallahassee, however, fans start beating the tom-toms as soon as the previous week's game is over and continue up to game time. Such a build-up might have had a bad effect on the keyed-up Seminoles, who often made mistakes and turnovers in the Florida game they might not have made in an ordinary game. A case in point was that October day in front of 64,000 fans at Florida Field.

That game turned out to be a great one for Gator senior fullback Jimmy DuBose, who rushed for 204 yards on 22 carries. He was just 14 yards short of Leroy "Red" Bethea's 218 yards

UF's Larry Brinson (#39) leads the way for Tony Green (#33) against FSU's Lee Nelson (#46) and Randy Coffield (#73).

gained against Chicago in 1930, but they were enough to lead the Gators to a 34-8 win over FSU. Jimmy Du, as his teammates called him, had the best day that any back had ever had against FSU. And although the Sarasota senior did not score a touchdown, his powerful running set up two running scores by Tony Green, one by Larry Brinson, and a pass from Jimmy Fisher to Wes Chandler. David Posey connected on four extra points and two long field goals. The only negative for the Florida win was a severe injury to quarterback Don Gaffney's left wrist. DuBose suffered a nasty gash right below his lower lip, but a trainer stopped the bleeding and enabled Jimmy Du to get back in the game for one of his best games ever.

Florida State scored late in the game on a pass from Clyde Walker to Mike Shumann and a two-point conversion from Shumann to Ed Beckman. FSU's great runner, Leon Bright, led his team in rushing with 62 yards on 13 carries, but an injured shoulder kept him from going all out, especially in blocking for the other ball carriers. The Seminoles had the hardiest player in

Billy McPhillips, who played both offense and defense for his injury-riddled team; ironically, he had caught passes from Jimmy Fisher, the Gator quarterback, when both had played high school football at Tampa King High School. The big problem for the Seminoles was their tendency to turn the ball over, losing four of seven fumbles and having two passes intercepted.

With his sixth straight win over FSU since returning to head up the Gators, Doug Dickey proved he was succeeding in building a powerful football team. The fact that his number-two quarterback, sophomore Jimmy Fisher could replace an injured Don Gaffney and lead the team to an impressive victory with 27 more points showed how deep the squad was. Dickey's staff, including the gifted Doug Knotts as defensive coordinator, worked well together. The mastermind behind Florida's great offensive showing that year was offensive coordinator Jimmy Dunn, the same Dunn who had quarterbacked UF to a win over FSU in the first game of the series (1958).

UF's band performs at halftime.

UF's football coaches

The Gators finished the regular season at 9-2, which was the best regular-season record of any UF team. The senior players became the first ones to make three straight bowl trips (Tangerine, Sugar, and Gator) and to beat Miami, FSU, and Auburn three straight times. In outscoring the opposition 302-104, they lost their only two games by a total of four points: 8-7 to North Carolina State and 10-7 to Georgia. The Gators did very badly in the Gator Bowl, losing to Maryland 13-0 for the first shutout of a Gator football team in 55 games; an estimated 25 million viewers saw the beginning of the game on television, but most probably left after they saw what a debacle it was turning out to be.

The Gators' Jimmy DuBose, whom offensive coordinator Jimmy Dunn called "the most complete player I've ever coached," became the SEC player of the year as he set a school rushing record. Linebacker Sammy Green became the Gators' 19th All-American player and continued adding to the reputation of linebackers who played for the team over the years.

The Seminoles finished their season at 3-8. Soon afterwards FSU fired head coach Mudra, who had compiled a 4-18 record in his two years there. He had alienated many FSU supporters by his aloofness, for example, in coaching the team from the pressbox during games. He had done much for the program, like providing better living quarters and a weight program for the players, but influential backers of the athletic program threatened to withdraw their support if he did not leave.

To replace him FSU hired Bobby Bowden, head coach at West Virginia and a former FSU offensive coach (1963-1965). Bowden had played football at Alabama as a freshman, then transferred to Howard College in Birmingham to play from 1949 to 1952. He stayed on as an assistant (1953-1954) before becoming head coach at South Georgia College (1955-1958) and then at Howard, (which had been renamed Samford) where he remained for several years (1959-1963), before Bill Peterson hired him on at FSU. After his three years at FSU, he became offensive coordinator at West Virginia (1966-1970), returning as FSU head coach (1970-1976). And thus began the highly successful Bowden era at Florida State University.

1976

Bobby Bowden Returns to Tallahassee

UF 33 - FSU 26

On January 12, 1976, Florida State made Bobby Bowden the university's seventh head football coach. The new Seminole head man would have five games to initiate his new system before Doug Dickey's Orange and Blue Gators came to town. After dropping his first three games, Bowden defeated Kansas State and Boston College and then turned his attention to his cross-state rival. The Gators were favored by a touchdown in this October battle and were ranked 12th by both the AP and UPI.

A warm mid-season evening found 42,803 fans on their feet for the kickoff in Doak Campbell Stadium. The Gators received and quickly scored on a David Posey field goal. When FSU fumbled deep at their end, Florida raised the count to 10-0 on a Larry Brinson 15-yard touchdown run. Early in the second period Dave Cappelen kicked a Seminole field goal, but Posey countered and the visitors were up 13-3. Florida State, with the versatile Jimmy Black at the controls, roared back. Black hit his first 12 passes and, mixing in a quarterback keeper, reached the UF 10. Rudy Thomas covered the remaining distance and FSU trailed by just three points. Before the halftime break FSU had forged ahead only to have the Gators re-take the lead in the first half's last ticks. Florida State's touchdown came on Black's 26-yarder to Kurt Unglaub. Then the Gators scored on Jimmy Fisher's throw to the brilliant wide receiver, Wes Chandler.

The Seminoles opened play in the game's final 30 minutes with an 80-yard march. Jimmy Black's passes and runs chewed up much of the ground, and the senior signal-caller plunged in

Coach Dickey and his coaches plan strategy.

from the two to put his team ahead again. But the see-saw tilt continued when Jimmy Fisher and Wes Chandler rolled to a quick six-pointer and a 27-23 lead. Following recovery of a punt which Chandler bobbled, Black completed a 45-yard strike to Jackie Flowers at the UF seven-yard-line. When Black was sacked and FSU missed a field goal, the Gators quickly increased their margin. Tony Green's long dash set up Earl Carr's short plunge and the Gators, with only seven minutes left in the game, led 33-23.

The Seminoles' chances for a comeback, already a long shot, were dealt a crippling blow on their next possession when the veteran Black suffered a concussion. Off the bench trotted Tallahassee freshman Jimmy Jordan. Jordan, who would be a major participant in the series before his career at FSU ended, came out firing. He hit Ed Beckman and Jackie Flowers, and Rudy Thomas ran to the Gator nine-yard-line. There the

UF defensive tackle Sylvester King (#73) looks over the program with coach Jim Niblack.

Garnet and Gold stalled, and Cappelen kicked a field goal. With five minutes to play UF led 33-26. When the Florida State defense held, Jordan had one last chance, but only 1:08 remained. The freshman found Beckman on the FSU 47 and Kurt Unglaub at the Gator 42 and then at the 22. With the home crowd howling for a score and with visions of a two-point conversion bringing victory, Jordan underthrew Beckman, who was alone in the end zone. Then he overthrew Jeff Leggett at the 15. On the 1976 game's last play, Jordan was sacked by old Tallahassee high school foe Michael DuPree. Florida's 33-26 victory was preserved.

Florida's offense produced 417 yards, much of it on the ground as Willie Wilder rushed for 98 yards and Tony Green for 90. Jimmy Fisher had a solid nine completions in 12 attempts for 139 yards in the air. Wes Chandler's four key catches, especially those just before the half, had a major impact on the contest's outcome.

For the Seminoles the big story was Jimmy Black, named the AP Southeastern Back of the Week for his efforts. Florida defensive chief Doug Knotts admitted that, "We couldn't contain Black's scrambling, and we couldn't cover Beckman one-on-one." The Tribe quarterback completed 14 of 17 for 211 yards and gained an additional 46 yards on the ground. The losing Noles amassed 507 total yards and 28 first downs, the latter a new mark for the series. After his team's first battle against the Gators, Bowden said, "I don't think you can ask for any better effort."

1977

The Noles Roll
FSU 37 - UF 9

In 1977 the Florida-Florida State game was switched to the end of the season. Florida State was 8-2-0 and 19th in the AP poll by the time the November date rolled around, while the Gators were 6-3-1. However, each team's last outing before their clash buoyed Gator hopes and depressed those of the Seminoles. With an 8-1 record, FSU traveled to California and was beaten badly by San Diego State 41-10. Florida's warm-up for the FSU game was a solid 31-14 victory over the Miami Hurricanes, a team which had earlier edged FSU 23-17. However, Gator faithful received some bad news when All-American receiver Wes Chandler, who had figured prominently in the 1976 game, came down with viral pneumonia and was out of the FSU game.

Those who tuned into ABC's regional telecast saw 62,563 at Florida Field watch the Seminoles kick off on a warm, cloudless afternoon. On UF's first possession Florida State's freshman noseguard Ron Simmons, one of the great names in Seminole football history, made his presence felt with two crunching tackles. Wally Woodham, who along with fellow Tallahassee Leon product, Jimmy Jordan, formed Bowden's novel quarterback tandem, opened with quick tosses to Kurt Unglaub and Mike Shumann (both also Leon grads) to move to the Orange and Blue 37. Then Woodham found Unglaub streaking down the east sidelines, lofted the ball, and watched his flanker juggle it, balance it on his fingertips, and cross the double stripes. Florida State led 7-0.

The Tribe scored again when Cappelen booted a 47-yard field goal to move the count to 10-0 at the quarter's whistle. Early in the second period Berj Yepremian countered for

FSU's Dave Cappelen (#1) attempts a field goal.

Florida with a three-pointer. When Woodham seemed to lose his touch, Bowden went to his back-up, Jimmy Jordan, who quickly fired a 46-yard strike to Roger Overby and then found Shumann for ten yards at the UF 26. Scott Hutchinson dumped Jordan for an eight-yard loss, and the visitors lined up third and 18 at the 31. With better protection, Jordan threw and Mike Shumann made a soaring grab at the Gator four-yard-line, a third-down conversion that may have been the game's key play. Two snaps later Jordan hit Overby for six, and FSU led 17-3. Before halftime Florida stalled twice in the Tribe end, but each time Yepremian got a field goal, the first from 50 yards out, the second from 41. At the midway pause in the action FSU was ahead 17-9.

The Seminoles received the kick-off to start the second half, and Jordan opened under center. At once Michael DuPree, who seemed to rise to the occasion against FSU, sacked Jordan, and a penalty set the Tribe on its own 12, third down and 30, a very long way to go. Jordan handed on a draw to Larry Key, and—amazingly—the senior rushing ace got 38

FSU's Mike Shumann.

to midfield. As Bowden said afterward about this vitally important play: "It was one of those situations where everybody in the stands knew you had to throw. Only you didn't." Although this drive ended in a missed field goal, Key's first-down effort made an enormous difference in field position and affected play in the entire third quarter.

Whenever Larry Key, a popular and skilled Seminole running back from 1974 to 1977, would carry the ball, fans would jangle their keys.

Florida's first second-half possession was quickly stifled by the defensive efforts of Ron Simmons and Willie Jones. On their next turn with the ball Florida State rolled goalward. Shumann got 18 on a reverse, and fullback Mark Lyles reached the 20-yard-line. Jordan faded back and hit Overby, who maintained his precarious balance and crossed the double stripes. FSU led 24-9.

As the third quarter moved to its conclusion, the Gators got a big break. Fielding a punt, Unglaub fumbled and UF's Garry Walker recovered at the FSU 30. Terry LeCount then came in with his orders from Doug Dickey and then began to move his team downfield. Tony Green quickly dashed to the nine and then got a tough two. LeCount kept to the five, where the Gators faced fourth down and goal. The Orange and Blue quarterback kept and knifed toward the goal line. Aaron Carter, a Gainesville High grad backing up the line for Florida State, slowed LeCount's progress at the two, and his fellow backer, Jimmy Heggins, stopped him one foot short of the touchdown.

FSU's Ivory Joe Hunter (#46), Ronald Simmons (#50), and Scott Warren (#80) close in on UF's Tony Green (#33).

Aaron Carter, nicknamed "A.C., " was a small, tenacious Gainesville native who came to FSU to lead the defense from 1974 to 1977.

Sometimes goal-line stands spur the offense to new heights. This was one of those times. Jordan set under center Gil Wesley with the Gator goal line 99 yards away and the UF defense, featuring the likes of David Galloway and David Little, determined to keep the Seminoles bottled up in their own end. But this was Jordan's day—and Shumann's and Overby's. The Tribe quarterback hit Overby, and Key then got to the FSU 25. Jordan found Shumann for 34 and Overby for 28. Mark Lyles completed FSU's long march from their own one-yard-line by scoring a touchdown. When the Gators fumbled Bill Capece's kickoff, the Tribe cashed in at once. Lyles and Key punched to the Florida 20. Jordan then lobbed his third scoring pass of the day, this one to Overby, whom cameras caught waving the ball triumphantly over his head in the end zone. The picture was Florida State's symbolic end to a decade of defeat and frustration. The Seminoles had won 37-9.

The 1977 edition of the series was the first Florida State blowout of the Gators and the most points FSU had scored on UF up to that point. The Seminoles' edge in yardage was 578 to 200 and in first downs 27 to 10. Jordan had 13 completions of 19 attempts for 240 yards and three touchdowns. Overby, Shumann, and Unglaub were balletic and glue-fingered. Larry Key carried 20 times for 145 yards to become the first Florida State player to rush for more than 1,000 yards in a season. And the Garnet and Gold defense led by Ron Simmons, Willie Jones, Aaron Carter, and Jimmy Heggins was magnificent as it limited the Gators to just three first-half field goals.

"Lovely, beautiful," were Bobby Bowden's words to an exultant crowd of 5,000 at Campbell Stadium in Tallahassee the evening after the victory, FSU's third win in the 20-year series and its first in the past ten years. "We're a good football team," he added. "I've been reluctant to say it, but now that the regular season is over, well, we're a good football team."

The Gators finished the season at a respectable 6-4-1. FSU's nine wins was the first time the team had nine wins in the regular season. They went on to beat Texas Tech in the Tangerine Bowl for a very satisfying 10-2 record.

1978

FSU—A Little Ornery
FSU 38 - UF 21

"Frustration" was a word that described both state university football teams as the 1978 game approached in late November. Florida was 4-5, and Gator supporters had begun to demand Doug Dickey's ouster. Florida State's frustration was less painful, but aggravating nonetheless. With a record of 7-3, the Tribe had just beaten a favored Naval Academy squad 38-6 only to wait in vain for the bowl bid many believed was deserved. Commenting on his team's failure to receive a post-season slot as the Florida struggle approached, Bowden said, "I hope it will make us a little more ornery."

The 1978 game in Campbell Stadium was to be the first at which the new FSU mascot, the horse Renegade and his rider Chief Osceola, appeared in the series. On a clear, cool night, 48,432 were in attendance in Tallahassee as FSU kicked off. One of the words most often used to describe team surges in football is "momentum." Never in the series has one half of football produced such a complete seizure of momentum by one eleven only to have it grabbed just as completely by the other team in an instant. Florida State was to win the first period 21-0, and, just as Seminole fans prepared to watch a massacre by their favorites, the Orange and Blue roared back to take the second quarter 21-0. When the bands began their halftime duel, the score was knotted at 21.

FSU's first period began quickly when Ron Simmons forced a fumble on the Gators' first snap that Mark Macek recovered at the six-yard-line. Mark Lyles went in for the FSU touchdown. Florida soon lost the handle again, this time at their own 22, and Lyles went in again. When Florida stalled and had to punt, Wally Woodham had the third FSU score three plays later on an aerial to Sam Platt.

Lightning changed sides of the field in the second 15 minutes. The Gators' John Brantley engineered a 64-yard march which ended with a David Johnson plunge for the tally. Florida kicked off, FSU's Lyles lost a fumble at his 25, and UF's Johnson scored his second touchdown in little more than a minute. A costly Seminole penalty for roughness aided the visitors for their next touchdown, which tied the score. What happened was that when a UF drive reached the FSU 23, on fourth down Dickey chose to have Berj Yepremian set for a field goal; the defense was called for roughing the kicker, and Florida had another chance. UF's Brantley took advantage of his opportunity, hitting Tony Stephens for 12 yards and a 21-21 halftime deadlock.

As the 1978 game's final 30 minutes opened, the crowd wondered which way momentum would move next. After each team's first possession in the third quarter, there seemed to be

U's Bill Capece kicks a field goal against UF.

Coach Dickey and his assistants, including Steve Spurrier (standing at right).

no momentum at all. On their second offensive turn of the half the Tribe began at their 29. Woodham's ball-control passes and line smashes by Mark Lyles and Homes Johnson advanced the ball to the UF seven-yard-line, from which spot the latter got the Seminole touchdown. For a time Florida appeared on its way to the equalizer, but FSU's Willie Jones and Ron Simmons decked John Smith for a huge loss. A short punt gave the Noles the ball near midfield. Seemingly bogged down on fourth down, Dave Cappelen gave Bowden a 10-point lead, 31-21.

For the balance of the contest the Seminole defense took charge and, for the fifth consecutive game, shut out the opposition in the second half. Scott Warren intercepted a Gator pass, and then Woodham's pass to Platt ate up 29 yards. At the one-yard-line, however, the Tribe quarterback's sneak was stopped inches short. But FSU's Warren intercepted again, this time at the Florida three-yard-line. When Lyles missed Woodham's handoff, the Garnet and Gold signal-caller kept and dove to paydirt. Florida State threatened one more time, but the game ended FSU 38 - UF 21.

After their explosive three-touchdown second quarter Dickey's men never really mounted another serious threat, primarily because an alert and tenacious FSU defense would not let up. Scott Warren, Ron Simmons, linebacker Reggie Herring, and, most of all, Willie Jones were outstanding. The Gator head coach paid the latter a tribute when he said, "Willie Jones was a fifth player in our backfield." Also memorable was the play of the FSU secondary led by Bobby Butler. That quartet passed its greatest test when Cris Collinsworth, the sensational Florida receiver, a threat to go the distance at any time,

UF's great receiver, Cris Collinsworth, later went on to star in the NFL with the Cincinnati Bengals.

wound up with just four catches for 45 yards and was not a factor in the game. Although FSU outgained the Gators only 416 to 357 and Florida had more first downs, the home team's defense was stingy when it counted, especially in the second half. Lyles had 100 yards rushing, and Woodham had 16 completions of 24 attempts for 179 yards.

One post-game revelation by Willie Jones may have helped inspire Tribe gridders. Lee McGriff, a Florida coach and former Gator standout on the field and in the classroom, had been a volunteer coach at Florida State in 1977. A rumor reached the Nole camp on the eve of the game that McGriff had said that Florida had more talented players than Florida State. Jones said, "Those things he said about us helped fire us up." Whatever did it, Florida State had accomplished a milestone in the series with the 1978 victory: it was the first time that FSU had won consecutive victories over the Gators.

The 1978 Florida State-Florida game was Doug Dickey's finale as Gator head coach. With a disappointing 58-43-2 record during his nine years (1970-1978) and never winning the Southeastern Conference Championship and having only one ranked team (1974 — 15th), Dickey had to go. Following the FSU game he was replaced by Clemson head man Charley Pell. After leading Jacksonville State to a 33-13-1 record over five years (1969-1973) and Clemson to an 18-4-1 record over two years (1977-1978), Pell chose to go to Florida to try to win an SEC championship and even a national championship for the Gators. Little did he know how disastrous his first Gator record would be; injuries would take their toll on a team that was playing what the NCAA considered the nation's toughest football schedule.

1979

Closer Than Expected
FSU 27 - UF 16

Could Florida State win three consecutive games from the Gators? Could FSU, 10-0, defeat Florida and complete their first undefeated regular season since entering major college football? Could the Gators, coached for the first time in the series by Charley Pell, and standing 0-8-1, spring the big upset and win their first game of the season? Would the Gators regard the FSU battle as their "bowl game" and derail Bowden's high-flying Tribe on their way to the Orange Bowl? These questions would be answered before 58,263 at Florida Field on Friday, November 23. The Friday-after-Thanksgiving date was chosen because the game was on national television.

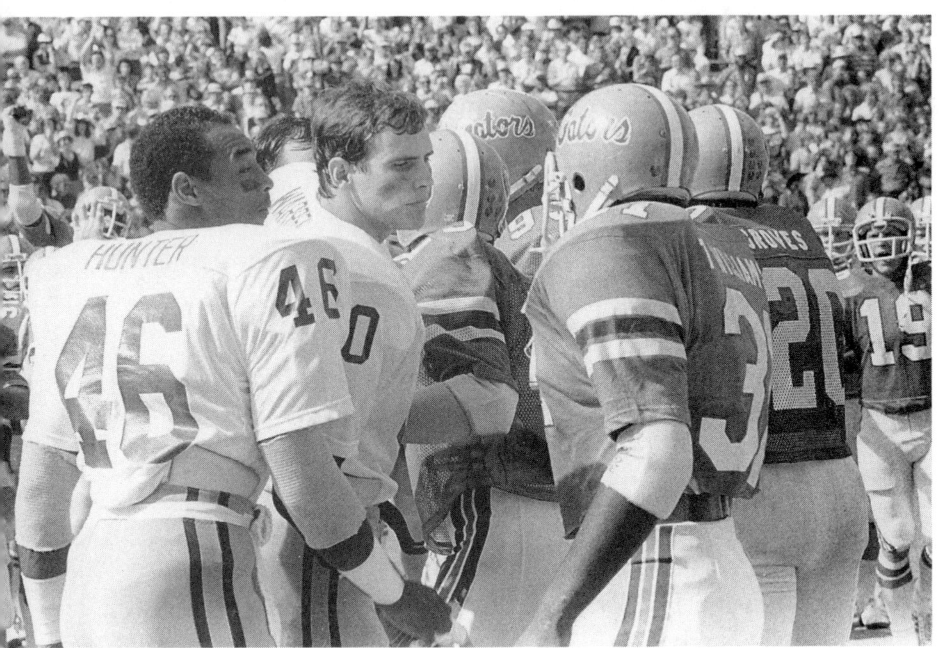

andshakes before the game begins.

UF's Tim Golden (#57) chases FSU's Jimmy Jordan (#15).

The 12:07 kickoff was shortly followed by a Tribe march engineered by Wally Woodham. Dave Cappelen's 42-yard field goal provided the first points on the board that afternoon, but the Gators lost little time in mounting their own threat. With diminutive Larry Ochab at quarterback, Florida reached the FSU 15 with the drive's big play a 39-yard Ochab-Cris Collinsworth aerial. At the 15-yard-line the FSU defense called a halt to the Gator advance. Ron Simmons, a consensus All-American in 1979, led a stand which forced Pell's team to try a field goal, but it sailed wide.

Late in the second period Bowden pulled Woodham, much as he had two years earlier, and went to his "fireman": Jimmy Jordan. Jordan completed pass after pass as the first half rolled to a close. Three of his yard-eating heaves were to tight-end Grady King. The touchdown came on a 22-yard throw into the corner of the end zone snagged by Hardis Johnson. At intermission FSU was up 10-0, but the stubborn, underdog Gators were holding on, and the heavily favored Seminoles were certainly not out of danger.

Coach Pell.

The first key play of the second half brought old high school teammates into hard contact. Jimmy Jordan faded to pass, trying to keep FSU's initial drive going, only to be sacked by Yancey Sutton, Gator linebacker and Jordan's high school mate and friend. Sutton's sack forced Florida State's Rohn Stark to punt from deep in Seminole territory. Then with Ochab throwing on almost every play (he would throw 54 passes in that game) the Gators got close enough for Brian Clark to sail a 39-yard field goal through the posts.

Then the Gator defense took charge and gave their offensive mates good field position and scoring chances. UF's Tim Golden picked off Jordan, and UF rolled to the FSU seven-yard-line. However, Ochab threw incomplete three straight times, and Clark missed a field-goal try. No sooner had the Seminole offense trotted on than Jordan was short circuited again, this time by Bill Fiorillo at the FSU 20. The Gator defender almost scored, barreling to the four-yard-line. Carl Prileau's plunge and Clark's point-after-touchdown gave the Gators a tie as the third period moved to its close.

After Jordan's two misfires and with the game's final 15 minutes beginning, Woodham returned to quarterback the Noles. Moving 80 yards, mostly on the ground, FSU's Michael Whiting and Mark Lyles tore through the Orange and Blue defenders. Lyles got the last 20 yards on a quick hitter through the right side of Florida's defense. When Pell's offense attempted to counter, Ron Simmons chased Ochab out of the pocket, forcing the Gator quarterback to fire on the run, and the Seminoles' Walter Carter intercepted. This play, a turning point, was the game's most controversial. ABC cameras picked up the ball being trapped by Carter, but there was no re-play and Carter's interception stood. Coach Pell angrily said later, "Six officials—and none of 'em saw it!" FSU reached the one-yard-line, and on fourth down Bill Capece hit a field goal to put FSU ahead 20-10. But the Gators would not roll over and die. When Terry Williams raced 51 yards to the FSU 27,the only significant Florida rushing action of the day, Florida seemed about to narrow the gap. At that point the Garnet and Gold defense said "no," and Clark missed his third field-goal try of the contest.

Once again the Gators came back, this time to a touchdown. Ochab's passes, aided by an interference penalty, moved his team downfield; the touchdown pass came on a catch by tight-end Chris Faulkner. Pell had the Gators try for a two-point conversion, but it failed. FSU, leading 20-16, expected the onside boot and easily took control of the ball. Aided by a penalty, FSU began to march and run out the clock from the Gator 40. Whiting and Lyles, behind a Seminole line opening big holes, alternated in blasting to the three-yard-line. From there Lyles got his second touchdown of the game to put Florida State ahead 27-16 with 1:10 left.

The game closed that way, and the Seminoles (later beaten by Oklahoma in the Orange Bowl) had an undefeated regular season and a third straight victory over their traditional foe. Florida, losing to Miami the next week, wound up 0-10-1. One memory of the 1979 struggle was its great length (3 hours and 12 minutes), the result of a combination of television commercials and Florida's 54 passes (32 incomplete).

Post-game stats revealed that FSU had only edged Florida 394 to 309 in total yardage thanks almost singlehandedly to Larry Ochab's 270 yards in the air for the Gators. Two Seminole ball carriers were well over the 100-yard mark: Lyles at 151 and Whiting at 123. Florida's ground game was so ineffectual that Seminole defenders could key on Ochab and his receivers. Perhaps the most important statistics in this 1979 renewal were on the defensive side. Seminole defenders intercepted Ochab five times and, as in 1978, effectively contained the great Cris Collinsworth, who caught only five passes. The '79 contest proved once again that one-dimensional offenses rarely win games against good, balanced teams. The winless Gators had played tough against the Seminoles and gave them some anxious moments as the men from Tallahassee rolled on to their perfect regular season. Ron Simmons went on to set FSU's season record for Most Tackles for a Loss (17), and Monk Bonasorte tied the school record for Most Interceptions in One Season (8).

1980

Seminole Seniors Go Four for Four FSU 17 - UF 13

This year would begin a tradition of having the two teams meet in the last regular-season game. In the early 1990s the two schools would consider meeting at an earlier point in the season because a loss in the last regular-season game would have a bad effect on the bowl picks and final rankings.

The 1980 season was another premier year for Bobby Bowden's Seminoles. By their December 6 meeting with Florida, FSU, 9-1, was ranked third nationally, and four voters had picked the Tribe number 1. Before the kickoff with Florida, the Seminoles had been invited to the Orange Bowl for the second straight year. After the Florida Gators' terrible 1979 campaign, Charley Pell's men had bounced back with a 7-3 run. Led by such future NFL standouts as Cris Collinsworth, David Galloway, James Jones, and David Little, Pell's second edition was a tough one. A fourth consecutive Florida State victory would not come easily, but a stellar class of FSU seniors, led by repeat All-American Ron Simmons, defensive back Bobby Butler, and great offensive tackle Ken Lanier (the latter pair both also future NFL stars) vowed to finish their collegiate careers without losing to their intrastate foe.

It was warm and sunny on December 6 when 53,772 crowded into Doak Campbell Stadium to watch the Seminoles and Gators duel for the 23rd time. FSU had not played a game in four weeks, a longer layoff than normal in order to have the game on national TV, and that long inactivity may have made the Seminoles somewhat sluggish at first. Florida State's first possession, with running-back Sam Platt leading the charge, stalled a little but ended with Bill Capece's 44-yard field goal. On this series Platt was injured and sat out the rest of the fray, which caused him to miss rushing for 1,000 yards that season by just 17 yards. The Gators came back, employing a two tight-end running game rather than Coach Pell's widely used four-receiver offense. An 88-yard march late in the first quarter paid off when quarterback Wayne Peace found tall, lanky ex-quarterback Tyrone Young on a 53-yard scoring toss.

In the second quarter the Gator defense stepped forward to try to take charge. David Little picked off a Rick Stockstill throw, and, when the Seminole defenders stopped UF, Brian Clark, who had been ineffective the previous year, booted a 38-yard field goal. Before the first half was history, Clark added another three-pointer, this one from 36 yards out. After 30 minutes of football, hometown fans and a television audience had seen Bowden's squad badly outplayed. Florida led 13-3.

The Seminoles brought the second-half kick-back to the 18 and promptly moved 82 yards to their first touchdown. Ricky Williams, subbing for the injured Platt, did the work on

UF players at practice.

UF's Wayne Peace throws over FSU's James Gilbert (#51).

the ground, while Stockstill's three passes to Hardis Johnson mixed up the attack. From the 19, Stockstill's last throw to Johnson brought the Tribe's deficit down to three. The fourth period, as Seminole fans proudly pointed out, had belonged to FSU that season, and the Nole defense had not given up a single point in the last period. As the last quarter opened, FSU and Stockstill were on the offensive. In a drive which covered 55 yards, the Stockstill-Johnson connection once again achieved results. In one of the most sensational catches ever made in the series, Johnson, falling out of bounds, gained 29 yards and kept Tribe momentum going. For the second time that afternoon the touchdown came from this aerial combo. When the Gator secondary blew coverage on Johnson, Stockstill found him, and the Tampa flanker went in on a 20-yard pass. FSU led 17-13.

Then the Florida State defense took over. The big plays, as the clock wound down, were an interception by Keith Jones, Arthur Scott's sacking of Wayne Peace on third down to deny the Gators a shot at a field goal, and Monk Bonasorte's tip of a Peace pass which Jones snagged with a diving interception. The final scoreboard tally was FSU 17 - UF 13. Florida State had won its fourth in a row.

The numbers, like the score, revealed an evenly played game. FSU had a narrow 275-257 lead in total yards. Hardis Johnson, with seven key catches for 107 yards and both Tribe touchdowns, was the game's outstanding performer. The five points that FSU's Bill Capece kicked gave him 104 points for the season, a new NCAA Division One record for kickers. After the game Gator head coach Charley Pell, paying tribute to the FSU seniors, said: "I've never been so happy to see a graduation take place. We should come and cheer at the FSU graduation ceremonies."

Three FSU seniors finished out their careers by setting school records. Ron Simmons had Most Tackles for a Loss (44) and Most Quarterback Sacks (25), while Monk Bonasorte had Most Interceptions (15), and Bobby Butler had Most Blocked Kicks (7). The Gators had two All-Americans that year: wide receiver Cris Collinsworth and linebacker David Little. Pell's teams were the first in college football history to go winless one season (1979) and then go on to a bowl at the end of the next season. Pell was named SEC Coach of the Year by both AP and UPI for what he accomplished that 1980 season: an 8-4 record and invitation to the Tangerine Bowl (where the Gators beat Maryland), and a ranking of 19th in the country. He had also won Coach of the Year in the Atlantic Coast Conference while he was at Clemson (1977 and 1978) and seemed on his way to building a Florida team that would consistently rank high in the polls.

UF's Johnell Brown gets ready to head down field.

1981

Charley Pell's Greatest Win
UF 35 - FSU 3

1981 was important for FSU sports because of the addition of Cecil "Hootie" Ingram as athletic director. The Tuscaloosa, Alabama, native had played football for Alabama (1951-1954) leading the nation in pass interceptions as a sophomore and later named to the All-SEC team. The fact that he also lettered in baseball at Alabama would help him understand the multi-talented Deion Sanders in the late 1980s. After graduation and a stint in the army, Ingram helped coach football at Bradenton's Manatee High in south Florida (1956), became the head football coach at Tuscaloosa Brookwood High School (1957), and later coached at Wake Forest, Virginia Tech, Georgia, and Arkansas, finally landing a head-coaching position at Clemson in 1970. Three years later he became assistant commissioner in the SEC. Eight years later he joined FSU and launched a successful, $10 million building program for athletic facilities at the school. The high caliber of men such as Ingram did much to attract athletes of the highest quality to FSU.

By the time the 24th renewal of the Florida-Florida State series came around at the end of the 1981 season, the Seminoles were, as Quarterback Rick Stockstill said, "physically and mentally tired." At mid-season Bobby Bowden's club had played one of the most demanding series of road games in the history of college football. On five consecutive weeks the Tribe had gone "on the road again," playing football powers: Nebraska, Ohio State, Notre Dame, Pittsburgh, and LSU. The Tribe had won three of those games, claiming wins over Ohio State, Notre Dame, and the Tigers of LSU, but had worn themselves out. There had followed a narrow loss to Miami, and, in their last game before going to Gainesville to end the long season, the Noles had been badly beaten by Southern Mississippi 58-14. The Gators, continuing to rebuild under Charley Pell, had lost to old rivals Miami, Auburn and Georgia, but were 6-4 and would be invited to play in Atlanta's Peach Bowl.

FSU had a week off after Southern Mississippi, and Bowden told the media, "My goal is trying to re-gather my football team." A crowd of 64,471, largely attired in Orange and Blue, gathered to watch Florida State's attempt to "re-gather." Florida launched an early drive, but the Tribe staved off disaster when Jarvis Coursey recovered a UF fumble. Trouble was not long in coming for FSU. The next time the Gators had the ball they went 63 yards to get on the board first. Wayne Peace rolled out behind an offensive line that gave him plenty of time, found tight-end Chris Faulkner, and Florida was ahead 7-0. Florida State came back with its own offensive that ended in a Mike Rendina field goal, and the Gator lead was cut to 4. Before the halftime festivities, Brian Clark, who had scored in the '79 and '80 games, nailed two field goals, from 50 and 41 yards out. Clark's first effort, booted through a swirling wind, was his 17th of the season and broke the SEC single-season field-goal record. After 30 minutes Pell's men were up 13-3. The Orange and Blue had outplayed the Seminoles in all facets of the game. The 1981 halftime score was exactly the same as in 1980, and a year earlier the Garnet and Gold had come back to win 17-13. Was another comeback possible? If so, Florida State would have to drastically mend its first-half ways.

Before many second-half ticks it was evident that another Seminole comeback was not to be. If Florida had outplayed the visitors in the first 30 minutes, they drubbed the Noles in the second half. Wayne Peace, who completed 20 of 33, had none intercepted and fired for four touchdowns, amassing 275 of the Gators' 437 yards of offense.

Florida drove early in the second half as Peace, who still enjoyed great protection, gained 39 yards on a throw to Spencer Jackson. This march concluded when, on fourth and one, the Gator quarterback faked into the line to James Jones,

This All-American punter for the Seminoles, Rohn Stark (1978-1981), went on to become a Pro-Bowl punter for the Colts.

pulled up, and hit tight-end Mike Mularkey all alone in the flat for a score. FSU continued to self-destruct. When they lost a fumble, Peace hit Johnnell Brown to make the score 28-3. Peace's coach summed the quarterback's game: "Today he was brilliant." In the fourth period Peace fired the last salvo in his arsenal, hitting Mularkey for a fourth touchdown through the air.

The 35-3 Florida victory was the series' greatest rout since the Gators had obliterated Florida State 49-0 in 1973. Seminole offensive coordinator George Henshaw had said before the game, "If we don't throw, we're going to lose." He

UF's Wayne Peace (#15) throws over UF's Russell Gallon (#78) and FSU's David Ponder (#85).

was right. FSU completed only 6 of 19 for 59 yards and threw three interceptions. “To lose your last three games is not encouraging,” Bobby Bowden told the press. The Seminole coach’s final words on his killer 1981 schedule and the outing against the Gators were simply, “We just flat ran out of gas.”

Understandably, Charley Pell was elated with his first victory in the traditional series. “I hate to be selfish,” said Pell,” but this is the greatest win I’ve had in football.” The Gators’ head man added, “I told Bobby that it’s about time he let us win.”

1982

Not Playing for a Tie
UF 13 - FSU 10

The two intrastate rivals that met before a record crowd of 57,369 at Doak Campbell Stadium for the 25th time were evenly matched. The Seminoles, 8-2 with wins over such teams as Cincinnati, Ohio State, Miami, and South Carolina, were the second-highest scoring team in the nation, with a 35.3 average. Part of that may have been due to Mike Kruczek, formerly a Pittsburgh Steeler quarterback, whom Coach Bowden hired to coach the quarterbacks. FSU sophomore tailback, Greg Allen, was the nation's leading scorer with 126 points. The expansion of Campbell Stadium added over 4,000 seats, and plans for a Sky Box for the major donors emphasized how seriously the university was taking its football program.

The Gators, 7-3 with wins over such teams as Miami, Southern California, Auburn, and Kentucky, were less sanguine. With unexpected losses to LSU and Vanderbilt and a 44-0 thrashing by Georgia, the Gators were not doing well. A recent NCAA investigation that had drawn attention to Coach Pell's alleged infractions while he was at Clemson was making some Gator fans question his leadership ability. The week before the game was full of tension for the Gators; one of their practices, which were closed to the public, was interrupted by an Indian riding into the Gator practice area, stopping before the players, and reading a list of charges against the team. After the Indian predicted disaster for some of the Gators, including quarterback Wayne Peace, he rode off into the night, making players wonder if that was an FSU plot or even a UF plot to motivate the players.

Fans expecting an aerial show from Airship Seminole and the Gators' Wayne Peace, who up to that point had passed for

1,783 yards and hit over 71% of his passes, were disappointed as the two teams slugged it out on a drizzling night. The Gators finally prevailed 13-10, thanks to the heroics of two second-stringers: Bob Hewko and Lorenzo Hampton.

When Gator starter Peace faltered in the first half, Hewko came in to direct a scoring drive to get his team back into the game and eventually on to victory. He rushed for a touchdown, and Jim Gainey kicked two field goals to give the Gators 13 points. Hampton had a career-high 138 yards on 23 rushes, and Neal Anderson had 103 yards on 13 carries, his third-straight 100-yard game. For the Seminoles Philip Hall kicked a field goal and Greg Allen ran in for a touchdown, giving FSU a total of 10 points. Ricky Williams rushed for 110 yards, and Greg Allen had 81 yards. The 10 points they scored was the lowest that year for the Seminoles.

With 52 seconds left in the game and FSU holding the ball at UF's 31-yard-line, Coach Bowden faced a fourth-and-nine and made one of those decisions that Sunday-morning

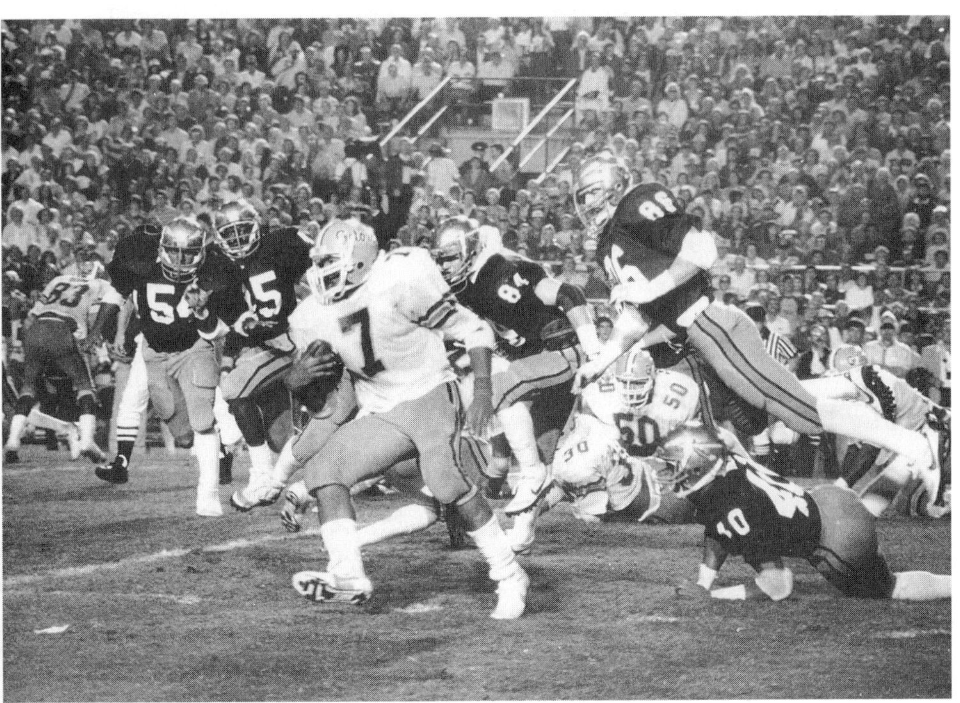

UF's Lorenzo Hampton (#7) runs toward the goal.

quarterbacks would discuss long and hard. Instead of trying for the tying field goal, Bowden decided to go for it all. When the Gators held on to win, some fans questioned his decision, but he later answered them: "A 48-yard field goal for a tie? I can't say that I've ever really played for a tie."

As the game ended, Hewko, who had lost his starting quarterback position to Wayne Peace after severely injuring his knee in 1980, wrestled the ball away from the referee, ran down toward the Gator end, and tossed it into the mass of UF students sitting there. It was his way of saying "thanks" to the many students who had supported him during the three years he had played for the Gators. Soon afterwards several hundred orange-and-blue fans spilled out onto the field and tore down one of the goal posts. The Seminole fans let them alone, probably wearied from the closeness of the game and the emotions it had taken out of them.

The game's heavy hitting took its toll on the players. The Gators lost their two starting defensive tackles (Roy Harris and John Whittaker) and had to use a freshman (Keith Williams) and a sophomore (Rodney Billet) in their place. The victory gave Charley Pell his first state championship in Florida and one victory over .500 in his career (23-22-1). Praising his team's determination and patience, Pell right after the victory called that game "the greatest win I've ever been associated with." The UF administration extended Pell's contract, which was to have run through the 1984 season, for two more years. After his depressing first season (0-10-1), he had led the Gators to three consecutive winning seasons and was about to lead them into their third consecutive post-season bowl game.

Coach Pell's Gators went on to lose to Arkansas 28-24 in the Bluebonnet Bowl, which put a damper on the enthusiasm that had been building since the late-season victories over Kentucky, Tulane, and FSU. Coach Bowden's Seminoles went on to beat West Virginia, where Bowden had coached before leaving for Tallahassee, 31-12 in the Gator Bowl and ended up ranked 10th in the nation with a fine record of 9-3. That bowl victory, the first-ever football game between the two schools, made up for bowl losses in the two previous seasons. FSU's Greg Allen, the MVP of the bowl game, ran for 138 yards and scored three touchdowns. It had been a great season for the Seminoles, especially with Greg Allen's 21 touchdowns and with an average of 465.8 yards/game, second best in the school's history before the explosive 1991 season.

One other note about the season-ending Gator Bowl. With just seven seconds left in the game, Bowden called time-out and instructed quarterback Blair Williams to pass to Jeff Bowden, a senior wide receiver who then caught his first pass in his five-year career. Jeff was the only Bowden son who did not attend West Virginia. The other three had attended the university where their father had coached before going to FSU.

In that game ending the 1982 season, the West Virginia Mountaineers wore on their sleeves the Gator Bowl logo, a Gator of course, but the Seminoles chose to wear "Gator Bowl, 1982" instead. They had had enough of Gators that season.

After the game UF's Ricky Easmon heads for the locker room.

1983

Reptiles Gig Indians
UF 53 - FSU 14

Florida Field had been expanded the previous year to a seating capacity of 72,000, which enabled the Gators to rank within the top ten in college football attendance. An extra 2,113 fans squeezed into the stadium on December 3, 1983, for a record crowd of 74,113, with some 26 million more watching on television; most expected a hard-fought battle as the Gators entertained the Seminoles for the 26th match between the two schools. What they got instead was a sound 53-14 whipping of the Seminoles as the Gators racked up the most points scored in a single game of the series. It was the most one-sided win in the annual match since UF's 49-0 victory in 1973.

The Gators dominated in every way: rushing yardage (297-149), passing yardage (212-108), total offense (509-257), total plays (84-54), and first downs (24-10). In a near-perfect game they scored on 11 of their 14 possessions with the running spread out among several backs: Neal Anderson (87 yards), Lorenzo Hampton (69 yards), Joe Henderson (62 yards), and John L. Williams (51 yards). Wide-receiver Dwayne Dixon caught seven passes for 94 yards to add some balance to the Gator attack, and Bobby Raymond kicked six field goals, which broke the UF record for a single game and tied the SEC and NCAA records. Peace rushed in for two touchdowns, Lorenzo Hampton for one, Neal Anderson for one, and substitute quarterback Donnie Whiting for one.

FSU quarterback Kelly Lowrey had five completions for 80 yards, including a scoring pass to Jessie Hester, and All-American Greg Allen carried 11 times for 87 yards, including one score. Those 87 yards increased Allen's season totals to

1,134 rushing yards, which made him FSU's single-season rushing leader, topping the 1,117 yards that Larry Key had gained in 1977.

However, as happened so often in the past, turnovers devastated the Seminole attack; FSU turnovers led to 20 of 23 points scored by the Gators in the first half alone. The FSU offense had some of Bowden's tricks, for example in an across-field lateral from Eric Thomas to Jessie Hester for a 61-yard kickoff return, but in the end the superior play of the Gators with good, solid football won the game. The Gator defense held the Seminoles to only 257 yards, the lowest all year for FSU.

Gator quarterback Wayne Peace, playing for the final time at Florida Field, became the SEC's career leader in passes completed (610), eclipsing UF great John Reaves, who had led the Gators from 1969 to 1971. The 6,901 yards Peace gained moved him up to the number 16th-ranked passer on the all-time NCAA list. Dwayne Dixon moved up to third on the Gator list of receptions, ending with 123 catches and moving past UF's 1980 All-American, Cris Collinsworth.

Various Gator mascots, including the huge gator in the background from the 1980 movie, "Alligator."

UF's John L. Williams (#22) blocks FSU's Brian McCrary (#43) for Wayne Peace (#15).

While Peace and Dixon excelled individually and together, most fans would probably remember little Bobby Raymond, all 5'8" and 170 pounds of him, as the one who had the stadium cheering. Fans might have forgotten that Raymond had been a walk-on who kicked 20 field goals that season in 23 attempts, breaking the school records (5 goals in one game and 18 goals in one season) of another great UF kicker, Brian Clark. Kicking those final six field goals was a fitting reward for his persistence and hard work.

After that loss, which millions saw on television, actor Burt Reynolds, a long-time supporter of the FSU program and a former player himself, telephoned Bowden and told him how terrible the team looked. Bowden thought Reynolds was referring to the team's play, but Reynolds was actually referring to the team's pants. Then Reynolds bought for the players sharp-looking gold pants with the Seminole symbol prominently displayed on the hip.

Florida went on to beat Iowa, the nation's third-ranked offense, in the Gator Bowl, 14-6, and finished with a 9-2-1 season, which enabled them to be ranked 6th in the Associated

Press and United Press International polls, the first time any Florida football team had finished in the Top 10. If they had scored just 11 more points at certain points in the season (2 more over Southern California, 8 more over Auburn, and 2 more over Georgia), they would have been undefeated and maybe the national champions. Miami was crowned the collegiate champion that year, with their only loss coming at the hands of the Gators, 28-3. Despite the NCAA investigation which had hung over the team all season, the players played solid football and richly deserved their high ranking.

Florida State University beat North Carolina, 28-3, in the Peach Bowl and finished a disappointing 7-5. What was most disappointing to Coach Bowden and Seminole fans was the team's defense that year, which allowed an average of 28 points a game. As if to remind the Seminoles how they had fared with their downstate rival the previous December, one less-than-classy Gator fan had a plane fly over Atlanta-Fulton County Stadium, where the Seminoles were beating the Tar Heels, and trail a banner that said simply, "Florida 53, Florida State 14." As if the Seminoles had to be reminded of that bitter loss.

One part of that season that FSU still has is what non-Seminole fans call the tomahawk chop. At the Auburn game that year several members of the FSU band, in an effort to urge on their team, began the monotone war chant and back-and-forward motion of the open hand that was meant to wave the Seminoles on toward the goal. Since then other fans have adopted the chant and hand slice, most notably the fans of the Atlanta Braves, the Washington Redskins, and the Kansas City Chiefs. While some Indians have been offended by some of the "Indian" rituals adopted by athletic teams, the Florida Seminoles have not been offended, partly because FSU's administration has worked with the Seminole tribe in developing its Indian traditions. And FSU has a top official of the Seminole Nation join the homecoming halftime festivities each year in Tallahassee as part of the administration's efforts to maintain a good working relationship with the school's namesakes.

1984

You Can't Pass in the Rain
UF 27 - FSU 17

If alligators are supposed to like a wet marsh, the Gators were right at home at Doak Campbell Stadium on the evening of December 1, 1984. The heavy rain that soaked players and fans alike made both teams change their game plans, and in the end the strong running game of the Gators prevailed in a 27-17 victory. The speed and quickness of Bowden's Seminoles, the nation's No. 1 scoring team with an average of over 37 points a game, might have prevailed on a clear night, but the mud and slippery conditions worked to the benefit of the hard-running Gators.

The 58,000-plus fans in attendance—another record for the stadium—and a national television audience saw Florida win its fourth straight over Florida State. The victory extended the Gators' win streak to nine, the second longest in the nation after Brigham Young's 23 straight, the only second nine-win season in UF history, and the longest winning streak for any Gator football team.

As so often in this series, miscues had much to do with the final outcome. FSU players fumbled eight times, losing three, and threw an interception. The Gators scored on passes from Kerwin Bell to Frankie Neal and John L. Williams, a run by Lorenzo Hampton, and two field goals by Bobby Raymond. The Seminoles scored on a Kirk Coker-Jessie Hester pass, an Eric Thomas-Pat Carter pass, and a field goal by Derek Schmidt.

For the FSU seniors, who were hoping that the 20th anniversary of the Seminoles' first victory over the Gators would be a lucky one for them, that loss meant that they had never beaten the Gators. For Coach Bowden it meant a long

UF's wide receiver Frankie Neal scores a TD.

year ahead; as he explained after the game, "This loss just means that there's 365 more days that I have to go making alibis to people. That's sickening. I have to go make all those speeches this spring and tell people why we lost to Florida. I dread that." He would also have to explain how the Gators in the previous four years had outscored the Seminoles 128-44.

The 1984 football season had been a tough one for Florida. The University of Florida fired head coach Charley Pell after the third game of the season for recruiting illegalities and named offensive coordinator Galen Hall the interim coach. Hall's team then proceeded to win the next eight games in a row and helped him become the head coach, a title he had for the first time without the "interim" at the FSU game. Although Southeastern Conference officials in Birmingham barred the Gators from playing in any post-season bowls, including the Sugar Bowl, for recruiting illegalities and stripped the SEC title from them, UF played with a determination that belied the critics. That FSU game meant the final Gator game for UF defensive coordinator Joe Kines and special teams coach Dwight Adams, both of whom would be let go for recruiting violations.

The two starting quarterbacks that day were stories in themselves. Both were walk-ons who had grown up in small north Florida towns 18 miles apart. FSU's Kirk Coker grew up in Perry and did well in football, but no recruiter came offering him a scholarship at the end of the season. He went to North Alabama for a year before transferring to Florida State, still without a scholarship. His persistence paid off when he substituted for the injured Eric Thomas in the Arizona State game and passed his team to a 52-44 victory.

Kerwin Bell grew up in tiny Day and played high school football in Mayo, hence the nickname "The Throwin' Mayoan." Bell went to the University of Florida without a scholarship and quietly bided his time. When injuries sidelined the four quarterbacks ahead of him, he calmly stepped in and slowly became the No. 3-ranked passer in the nation and the SEC's passing leader.

Because of NCAA probation, the Gators could not compete in any bowl games, but they still had hopes for a national championship because of their record (9-1-1) and the difficulty of their schedule, but it was not to be. They were ranked third in the Associated Press poll, the highest ranking yet of any Gator football team; the nation's sportscasters and sportswriters voted in that poll. *The New York Times* computer poll considered teams' won-loss record against the various teams and ranked the Gators Number One in the country. *The Sporting News* examined the teams' schedules and consistency of play and also ranked the Gators first in the country. AP and UPI both named Galen Hall Coach of the Year.

Florida State tied Georgia 17-17 in the Florida Citrus Bowl and finished up the season at 7-3-2; for Bowden, who had never before had a tie game, two ties in one season seemed very odd. The Seminoles ended up 17th in the AP poll and 20th in the UPI, which also ranked the Gators 7th. FSU's Gene McDowell, coach of the linebackers, would move on to become head coach of the University of Central Florida football team.

UF President Marshall Criser and Coach Galen Hall hold the New York Times National Championship Trophy and the 1984 SEC Championship Trophy.

1985

The Gators' "Bowl" Game
UF 38 - FSU 14

What to call the annual match-up between UF and FSU became something of an issue in 1985 when *The Orlando Sentinel* came up with several suggestions, including "The Sunshine Sizzler," "Cracker Clash," "The Swamp Slosh Bowl," and "The Zest Bowl." In any case, the Gators called it their "bowl" game since NCAA probation did not allow them to compete in any post-season games. The Gators entered the game at 8-1-1, ranked sixth in the nation, and relying on sophomore signal-caller Kerwin Bell. The Seminoles, ranked 12th in the nation at 8-2, would rely on freshman quarterback Chip Ferguson. Another record crowd, 74,461, was at Florida Field to see which of the fairly even teams would prevail. As happened so often in the past, the records coming into the game counted for little. FSU came in with impressive wins over South Carolina (56-14) and Western Carolina (50-10), whereas UF entered in after a loss to Georgia (24-3) and a squeaker win over Kentucky (15-13). The Gators had been ranked first in the nation before the loss to Georgia.

The Seminoles knew that Florida had won 19 straight games at Florida Field, but maybe something would happen to stop that streak. It was not to be, though, as the Gators soundly beat them 38-14. Florida quarterback Kerwin Bell threw for three touchdowns as he completed 14 of 22 passes for an impressive 343 yards. He connected on two scoring passes to Ricky Nattiel and one to Frankie Neal; Jeff Dawson kicked a field goal, and Neal Anderson ran in for two touchdowns as he joined Jimmy Dubose to become the only Florida running backs to rush for more than 1,000 yards in one season.

Anderson's two rushing touchdowns boosted his record total to 32. Bell's 21 passing touchdowns for the season increased his career total to 37, enough for second on the Gators' all-time passing list ahead of Steve Spurrier and behind John Reaves, who passed for 54 touchdowns in his career. For FSU, Deion Sanders returned a punt for a touchdown, and quarterback Chip Ferguson ran in for the other score.

Although the Seminoles had lost to the Gators five years in a row, one Gator, in a weird turn of events so common to this rivalry, had lost to FSU. When junior safety Adrian White had played for Southern Illinois as a freshman in 1982, his team lost 59-8 to the Seminoles in Tallahassee. He later trans-

SU's Deion Sanders (#2) scores a touchdown and Terry Robinson (#15) celebrates.

ferred to Florida, sat out in 1983, and played well for the Gators for the past two seasons, enjoying the victories over the instate rival a little more than those who had never been beaten by FSU. UF led the series 21-6-1 after that fifth straight victory.

After the game ended, the Gator fans at Florida Field refused to leave. They knew that was the last game of the season for the NCAA-penalized team, and they wanted to express their appreciation for a job well done under trying conditions. The seniors, who had joined their teammates in the locker room, returned to the playing field and gathered together at midfield to receive the accolades of the fans. When the applause died down, senior spokesman Neal Anderson expressed the feelings of the entire team when he said to the crowd, "I'd like to thank you for all your support this year. Without you, it wouldn't have been possible."

UF's Neal Anderson says "goodbye" to Gator fans.

The Gators celebrate their victory.

That win enabled the Gators to be the first Florida team to win nine games in three consecutive seasons and tied the previous year's record (9-1-1) for the school's best season record. Coach Galen Hall, who had his UF contract extended through the 1990 season, became the first coach in SEC history to go unbeaten in his first 17 games and tied the record for most victories (17 overall and 10-1 in the SEC) by a coach in the league in his first two seasons. Among the Gators playing their last game for the Orange and Blue were running backs Neal Anderson and John L. Williams, punter Ray Criswell, and All-America linebacker Alonzo Johnson. Anderson was the only UF player to rush for more than 3,000 yards in his career, and his 14 100+-yard games and 32 career touchdowns were school records.

The Seminoles went on to beat Oklahoma State 34-23 in the Gator Bowl and ended up ranked 15th by the AP and 13th by the UPI. Their final record of 9-3 promised good things for the following season, especially since the Seminoles had redshirt freshman Sammie Smith moving up to the varsity to replace another standout, tailback Tony Smith; freshman Chip Ferguson, who completed 20 of 43 passes in the Gator Bowl game for a career-best 338 yards and two TDs, was getting better each game. FSU's seniors Jamie Dukes, John Ionata, Todd Stroud, and Isaac Williams would leave school without ever having beaten the Gators, but the newer players had high hopes. When lineman Dukes, whom FSU offensive coordinator Wayne McDuffie called "the best player I ever coached," started in the Gator Bowl game, his 48th start was the most of any FSU player in history.

Coach Bowden was looking forward to next year's match with his downstate rivals; as he explained after his latest loss, "If we ever beat Florida, there's going to be a celebration that lasts for weeks." He needed to get back on the winning ways against his Gainesville nemesis. After his first loss to the Gators in 1976, his first year at FSU, Bowden had won four in a row before starting his five-year drought against UF. He would have a long winter and spring answering the inevitable "How come?" questions from the Seminole fans and trying to figure out how to "Gig the gators" again.

The Gators, whose probation prevented them from playing in a post-season bowl and from being on the UPI list, were ranked 5th by the AP; that ranking meant that the Gators were the only team in the nation to finish within the top six spots in the AP poll in the previous three seasons. The Gators were looking forward to the next football season; if they could keep their program clean, the Gators would be eligible to play in a bowl at the end of the 1986 season. They knew the NCAA-limit of 75 scholarships, 20 lower than the standard, would hurt, but they were hoping they could find those few good players who could give them a winning season, especially against their Tallahassee rival.

1986

"Arriving to us is beating Florida" UF 17 - FSU 13

Many of the 60,307 fans, a record for Tallahassee's Doak Campbell Stadium, expected an FSU victory that November night in 1986 and an end to the five-game losing streak to the Gators. True, the weather was nasty as rain came down all through the game and made the field hard to run on, but the Seminoles were the fifth-best scoring offense in the nation, averaging over 35 points a game, and they had a 44-8 record in home night-games. They were entering the annual grudge match with a respectable 6-3-1 record, and many thought the team had finally arrived, especially after recently beating Southern Mississippi 49-13 and losing only to No. 1 Miami, No. 4 Michigan, and No. 6 Nebraska. Coach Bowden disagreed: "Arriving to us is beating Florida."

The NCAA penalties imposed on the Gators were definitely taking their toll. Scholarship restrictions had cut into the depth of the team, and some players, like FSU's Sammie Smith, had chosen the Tallahassee team soon after the NCAA put the Gators on probation. A 10-3 loss to Kentucky two weeks before the FSU game ended Florida's plans of going to the Hall of Fame Bowl, threatened to give the Gators a losing season for the first time since the disastrous 0-10-1 season of 1979, and once again made the FSU match their "bowl" game.

In this particular game the Seminoles played a good game against the Gators for three-and-a-half quarters. Derek Schmidt kicked two field goals, and Sammie Smith ran in for a touchdown to give FSU a 13-10 lead before the decisive fourth quarter. Freshman Smith also ran for a 47-yard touchdown in the

UF's Kerwin Bell (#12) looks over the line of scrimmage.

third quarter, but a holding penalty nullified that go-ahead score. Fans with a long memory pointed out that this game was the 20th anniversary of the infamous Lane Fenner call in which the go-ahead score was nullified by a bad call. Penalties hurt both teams a great deal. FSU set a school record with 15 penalties for 116 yards called against it. For the Gators, Octavius Gould rushed for a touchdown, and Jeff Dawson kicked a field goal. The score was FSU-13, UF-10 until midway in the fourth quarter. Facing a fourth-and-10 at the Gator 29, Coach Bowden decided to go for the field goal and sent in Derek Schmidt for a third field goal from 46 yards out. When the ball was snapped and set down for the kick, Gator back Louis Oliver, all 6'2" and 215 pounds of him, leaped up from the middle of the line and blocked it.

Florida took over at its own 40. Coach Galen Hall sent in third-string tailback Wayne Williams to run the ball, first 11 yards, then 9, then 2; Bell scrambled for 3 before Williams resumed his ball-carrying: 13 yards, then 2, and 2 again. With third-and-six at the FSU 18 and only 3:57 remaining in the game, many in the stands thought that Jeff Dawson would come on to kick the tying field goal. But Coach Hall did not send Dawson in to kick the field goal. Instead, quarterback Bell took the snap, dropped back, and lofted a pass to Ricky Nattiel, who caught it in the end zone for the winning touchdown. Final score: UF 17, FSU 13.

FSU had played a decent game, gaining 248 yards on that wet night, 47 yards more than the Gators. Freshman Seminole Sammie Smith rushed for 116 yards on 24 carries and gave a glimpse of what a great career he would have at FSU. For UF, quarterback Bell hit on only eight of 17 passes for a career-low of 65 yards, but his final toss to Nattiel, Ricky's last catch as a Gator, would be one both of them would long remember.

Phrases like "a hex on the Seminoles" and "the Gators being favored by the Gods of Football" began appearing after the game in the media. Reporters needed something to explain UF's sixth victory in a row. One Seminole fan swore that the rain stopped just as Bell faded back to loft the winning touchdown pass to Nattiel. But surely hexes and meteorological miracles don't exist in football!

As happened so often in the past, young men who had played together on high school teams found themselves competing against each other in the UF/FSU game. And after they finished their college eligibility and played in the National Football League, loyalties might change once again. For example, cornerback Martin Mayhew, who had excelled for the Seminoles for four seasons (1983-1986), found himself on the same team, the Washington Redskins, with former Gator Wilber Marshall and competing against former teammate Deion Sanders of the Atlanta Falcons.

Florida finished its season that night with a disappointing 6-5 record, but at least they had beaten the Seminoles one more time, and Coach Hall could revel on the post-season banquet trail by describing how the Gators had bounced back from four straight early-season losses to dramatically beat the big three: Auburn, Georgia, and FSU. Florida also announced it was hiring Bill Arnsparger, successful LSU football coach, to be its new athletic director.

FSU would go on to beat Indiana 27-13 in the All-American Bowl at Birmingham on New Year's Eve. Tailback Sammie Smith rushed for 205 yards and scored two touchdowns to win Most Valuable Player honors. FSU, which the UPI ranked 20th, finished the season at 7-4-1, and its bowl victory gave it a 4-0-1 record in its last five bowl appearances. Coach Bowden, who was being considered for the head coaching position at Alabama, withdrew his name from consideration. He was happy at Florida State, and Seminole fans were obviously delighted with his brand of wide-open football.

1987

Bowden Breaks the Jinx
FSU 28 - UF 14

On a beautiful, sunny November afternoon in 1987 the 9-1 Florida State Seminoles took the field in Gainesville to do battle with Galen Hall's orange-jerseyed Gators, coming in at 6-4. FSU's lone loss was a 26-25 heartbreaker to the Miami Hurricanes in its fifth game. The Gators had see-sawed back and forth in 1987, beating Alabama at Birmingham, but dropping games to traditional rivals Auburn and Georgia. Hall's men were led by freshman offensive sensation Emmitt Smith and senior quarterback Kerwin Bell on offense and hard-hitting safety Louis Oliver on defense. Florida State's big offensive standouts were QB Danny McManus and running backs Sammie Smith and Dexter Carter. On defense Deion Sanders, Stan Shiver, Paul McGowan, and Odell Haggins had played tough all year. Comparative scores, often very unreliable, seemed to give Bowden all the advantages in this one. FSU had whipped Auburn 34-6, while the War Eagles had handed the Gators a 29-6 defeat.

Florida State's Derek Schmidt kicked off, and UF could only reach its own 21. On the opening snap Emmitt Smith charged 43 yards to the FSU 37 and almost went the distance. But the Garnet and Gold defense, led by Shiver's sack of Bell, forced Hall's team to punt. McManus and his mates moved smartly to the UF nine-yard-line, the Gators held, and Schmidt kicked a field goal to give his team a 3-0 advantage.

Momentum, aided by a Gator interception of McManus, switched sides. Bell began handing off to Smith again and again, and the Pensacola freshman did the job, eventually taking it in from the five-yard-line. When Florida State went three and out, Rick Tuten's punt was blocked, and Smith had only

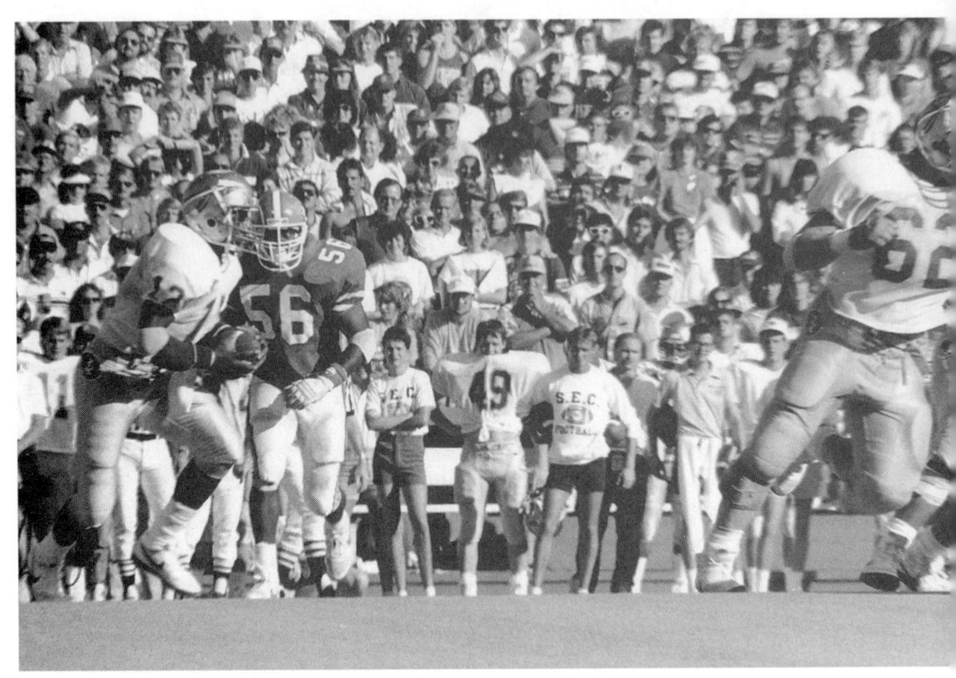

UF's Clifford Charlton (#56) chases FSU's Rick Tuten (#12) while Jason Kuipers (#62) blocks.

FSU's Eric Hayes (#78) gets by UF's Clifton Reynolds (#81) and focuses on Emmitt Smith (#2

nine yards to cover this time. He did the job at once, and Florida led 14-3. The pro-Gator crowd had visions of a major upset in the making. After six consecutive losses, Bobby Bowden was beginning to think that he was jinxed by the Gators.

For a time the situation did not get much better. The Seminoles drove, only to have the usually reliable Schmidt miss a field goal. Most of the second period was a hard-hitting defensive standoff, but the Tribe did roll close enough to twice allow Bowden to send Schmidt out to seek redemption. He was redeemed as his two field goals, from 23 and 53 yards out, made the halftime score 14-9 in Florida's favor.

The Seminoles took the second-half kickoff and began to move forward. On the second play, Sammie Smith scooted 39 yards, and only a tackle from behind by Louis Oliver averted the touchdown. When the march stalled, Schmidt hammered through his fourth field goal, this one from 37 yards out.

On their next offensive series the Tribe, grinding it out on the ground again, drove goalward. Eating up ground and the clock, they reached the Gator one-yard-line when Dayne Williams, used all year by Bowden for goal-line smashes, plunged in. Edgar Bennett covered the three yards for a two-point conversion, and Florida State led 20-14. This game's final period was more of the same. The FSU defense allowed the Gators almost nothing, and Bowden's offensive 11, sticking largely to the ground (McManus threw only three times in the second half), scored one final touchdown as Williams bucked in from the one. McManus flipped to Herb Gainer for the two-point conversion, and Florida State had a 28-14 victory. Bowden's six-game string of losses had been broken at last.

Florida State out first-downed UF 26-11 and had an enormous 411-207 margin in total yards. Emmitt Smith carried 20 times for 100 yards, but two Garnet and Gold ball carriers finished ahead of the Gator frosh. Sammie Smith had 116 yards, while slashing runner Dexter Carter had 111. After a very even first half, made even in large part by Seminole miscues, the second 30 minutes was almost all FSU. A tenacious defense and—unusual for the pass-happy Seminoles—a hard-driving running game put this renewal in the Garnet and Gold win column.

This was not the year's final game for either squad. Galen Hall's men traveled to Hawaii, where they were narrowly edged by UCLA in the Aloha Bowl and finished even at 6-6. With his 1,341 yards that season Emmitt Smith set the Florida record for rushing yardage. Florida State won an exciting Fiesta Bowl from Nebraska and wound up 11-1 and second nationally in both the AP and UPI polls.

Kerwin Bell finished his Florida career by setting numerous records, including 7,585 career passing yards, which placed him second to John Reaves in career total offense. More remarkable than the figures he compiled over four years was the determination to succeed in the face of overwhelming odds. Having walked on at Florida Field with no scholarship (only Valdosta State had offered him one), he found himself without a jersey and ranked number eight on the depth chart. When the equipment manager gave him number 12, after its wearer had chosen another number, Bell realized that his idol, Roger Staubach, also wore that number and took it with enthusiasm. Bell slowly worked himself up the depth chart until he became the starter and proceeded to rewrite the Florida record book, before going on into the professional ranks and a coaching career.

1988

Two Straight for the Noles
FSU 52 - UF 17

Just after Thanksgiving in 1988 the Florida Gators drove northward to do battle with Florida State, fully aware that the Seminoles had won 21 of 23 games since their 1986 loss to the Gators at Doak Campbell Stadium. Galen Hall's Gators had begun the season with a bang, winning their first five games. Then they dropped their next four before defeating Kentucky in their warm-up for the Noles. The UF offense was led by their great running back, Emmitt Smith, but even Smith could not make up for overall inconsistency and shaky quarterback play.

Bobby Bowden's Seminoles, ranked number one in the nation in the pre-season AP poll, opened with a disaster: a 31-0 pasting by the Miami Hurricanes. Not discouraged by the Miami rout, FSU had won nine straight (including the famous "puntrooskie" game against Clemson) by the time the Gators came to town. Leading the Garnet and Gold were quarterback Chip Ferguson, running back Sammie Smith, and a tough defense revolving around Odell Haggins, Eric Hayes, and a rather outspoken defensive back named Deion Sanders. Both squads were on their way to bowl games in 1988. FSU was to duel the Auburn Tigers in the Sugar Bowl; the Gators were to play Illinois in the All American Bowl.

Early in the 1988 renewal the teams traded touchdowns. FSU got on the scoreboard first when Chip Ferguson fired to Lawrence Dawsey, who stumbled and reeled into the end zone determined not to be stopped short of the double stripes. Florida got a 46-yard kickoff return from Tony Lomack, another of the many Tallahassee Leon prep stars to play for the Gators. Emmitt Smith completed the march with a tying one-yard plunge.

UF's Trace Armstrong (#93) chases FSU's Chip Ferguson (#5).

Before the initial quarter had ended, however, Chip Ferguson had broken the tie by adding two more touchdown passes. He found tight-end Tom O'Malley for the first and then Sammie Smith on an eight-yarder. John Hadley's interception at the UF 24 set up the last of the three touchdowns. After 15 minutes, FSU had a 21-7 lead. After 28 first-period points the offenses slowed down, and the second period saw the teams trade field goals: one by Bill Mason from 19 yards for Florida State and one by John David Francis from 24 yards for UF. By intermission the Seminoles led 24-10.

After the bands left the Campbell Stadium turf, Bowden's offense, defense, and special teams took over with each claiming a touchdown by the time the third period had ended. The first unit to produce was the special teams. Tim Corlew drilled a 53-yard punt to Kerry Watkins, who fumbled at his ten-yard-line and retreated into the end zone groping for the ball, only to have FSU's Marion Butts fall on the rolling pigskin for the touchdown.

FSU's Phil Carollo (#81), Jason Crain (#38), and Corey Senior (#57) close in on UF's Willie McClendon (#5).

The FSU defense halted Florida, and a 60-yard march saw FSU's Dayne Williams move the score to 38-10. By then nothing was going right for Hall's men. On the first play after the kickoff Orange and Blue quarterback Kyle Morris, badly harassed all day, threw hard but saw the ball tipped by linebacker Anthony Moss into the hands of noseguard Odell Haggins. Haggins, not to be denied his moment on the scoreboard, dragged two Gators 11 yards for the touchdown.

Gator fans began to leave, and the predominantly Seminole home crowd chanted "so long, bye bye," through a final stanza that saw the teams trade touchdowns. FSU scored when Peter Tom Willis relieved Ferguson and hit Terry Anthony. Willie McClendon got the final Florida tally, and the game ended FSU 52, UF 17. The 35-point victory was Florida State's most one-sided victory in the series.

The Garnet and Gold outgained Florida 414 yards to 183 and had twice as many first downs. Emmitt Smith was held to only 56 yards in 15 runs, while Gator quarterbacks, with miserable protection, had a long day, completing six of 20 attempts

UF's Emmitt Smith (#22) leaps over UF's Ernie Mills (#14) and away from FSU's Tracy Sanders (#16).

with only 73 yards and two interceptions. For FSU, Ferguson was 10 of 16 for 131 yards and those three early scores. In the battle of the Smiths, Sammie decisioned Emmitt 109 yards to 56.

The 1988 meeting with the Gators brought Bobby Bowden's sixth victory in 13 games and was a prelude to a Sugar Bowl-win and a 3rd place ranking by both wire service polls at season's end, a remarkable ending for a team that many had dismissed after that initial, early-season loss to Miami. That Sugar Bowl game was the seventh straight bowl appearance for the Seminoles and the 10th in Bowden's 13 years at FSU. The Gators finished the year at 6-5, but did have defensive back Louis Oliver and defensive end Trace Armstrong named to the All-American team.

1989

Victory on the Arm of Peter Tom FSU 24 - UF 17

On December 2, the 8-2 Florida State Seminoles, having lost their first pair and won their next eight, rode the bus down the road to Gainesville. At Florida Field they would meet the 7-3 Florida Gators, a team whose season had led to rising demands for the ouster of their coach, Galen Hall.

A crowd of mostly Gator fans saw FSU strike with just over three minutes remaining in the first quarter. Peter Tom Willis, completing the most productive single season in the history of the pass-oriented Seminoles, hit wide receiver Terry Anthony with a 62-yard bomb. Up to that time there had been little to cheer about in the game for either squad and much to deplore. Both teams were embroiled in on-field fights, and the first 15 minutes were marred by numerous penalties. By halftime UF had been whistled for 104 yards in infractions while Florida State had run up 98 penalty yards. The end-of-game totals for both teams were 258 yards.

Before the first period ended, the Gators had rolled 44 yards, and John David Francis's 46-yard field goal had brought the score to 7-3. The first points in the second quarter were also generated by the home team. A 61-yard drive culminated in a three-yard reverse run by wide-receiver Stacey Simmons. The visiting Noles were not long in responding. Moving 66 yards in 12 plays, the march ground to a halt at the Florida eight-yard-line. Richie Andrews was called on, and his 24-yard field goal tied the game at 10-10, which is where the score remained when the halftime whistle sounded.

UF's Mark Murray (#54) and Phillip Johnson (#64) and FSU's Edgar Bennett (#22) chase a loose ball.

Peter Tom Willis, who would pass for 319 yards in the game, his sixth 300-plus game of the season, engineered a 63-yard, six-play drive to give his squad the lead for good. The key drive-sustaining play of this third period march came on second down and 26 when Willis hit fullback Edgar Bennett on a screen, and Bennett picked up 38 yards. While not the same kind of play, Bennett's screen pass reminded spectators of Larry Key's long draw-play to keep a drive alive in the 1977 struggle. The scoring toss following Bennett's play was a 22-yarder from Willis to Bruce LeSane.

FSU's Dexter Carter (#13) leaves teammate Chris Hall (#41) and UF's Greg Baldwin (#51) behind.

The Gators mounted a potentially tying threat early in the final 15 minutes of play, reaching the FSU 15. There Francis missed a field goal, and the Garnet and Gold followed with an 80-yard drive to put this game in the W column. Willis had a third touchdown pass of the day, a 10-yard throw to tight-end Dave Roberts. The Gators did get one late touchdown with their great running back Emmitt Smith crossing the stripes from two yards out. The Orange and Blue had one last chance

FSU's Peter Tom Willis (#4) passes while teammates Kevin Mancini (#67) and Tony Yeomans (#70) block and UF's Mark Murray (#54) closes in.

with just under a minute remaining, but the Tribe's prevent defense killed the opportunity. The final count in this 32nd renewal was 24-17, Florida State.

The statistical rundown was as even as the score. FSU had a slight edge in both first downs and total yardage, most of the latter due to Willis' stellar numbers: 20 of 32 for 319 yards. The Gators' major effort was on the ground, where Emmitt Smith had his greatest day against the Seminoles. The underclassman, who would turn pro before the 1990 season, carried 30 times and gained 153 yards.

Bowden's third consecutive victory over the Gators and Coach Galen Hall kept the Seminoles' successful season moving ahead. The Seminoles went on to the Fiesta Bowl, where they defeated Nebraska and wound up second in the UPI's final poll and third on the AP's list. The University of Florida would begin the following football season with several new faces, beginning at the top with a new president: Dr. John Lombardi. For its football coach the school terminated Coach Hall's stay at UF and replaced him with a man who had made his mark in the Florida-Florida State series on the field. He would now try to do the same from the sidelines. His name was Steve Spurrier.

1990:
Offense Is the Name of This Game FSU 45 - UF 30

When the Garnet and Gold Florida State Seminoles and the Orange and Blue Florida Gators lined up on December 1 for the 33rd edition of their intense grid rivalry, two coaches faced each other for the first time. Two of the most famous names in the history of sports in the Sunshine State—Bobby Bowden and Steve Spurrier—led the two explosive elevens they had created onto the natural turf of Doak Campbell Stadium. A stadium record crowd of 63,190 was on hand to see the game.

The Seminoles were 8-2, having lost on back-to-back Saturdays at mid-season to Miami and Auburn. Tallahasseean Casey Weldon, who would quarterback the Tribe, would be aided by brilliant wide receiver Lawrence Dawsey and versatile running backs Amp Lee and Edgar Bennett. Spurrier's troops would be commanded by quarterback Shane Matthews, later to be named SEC player of the year. The highly touted UF defense would be led by Huey Richardson, Richard Fain, and, coming home to play, Leon star Brad Culpepper and Godby ace Will White. The Gators were 9-1, and a victory over Florida State would bring Florida its first 10-win season in the long history of football in Gainesville.

Bobby Bowden has the reputation of being a "riverboat gambler," possibly the most unpredictable coach in American football. Two plays into the game the wily Seminole chief enhanced his reputation. Lining up on his 24, Casey Weldon faded, watched number 29, Lawrence Dawsey, break by Fain, and threw deep. Dawsey hauled it in and raced to a 76-yard touchdown. Before the crowd had settled into their seats, FSU led 7-0.

On the Gators' first offensive play Willie McClendon was drilled by Bill Ragans, and Howard Dinkins recovered the fumble for FSU. The turnover led to a 47-yard Richie Andrews field goal, and—with only 2:03 gone—the Tribe was ahead by ten points. Florida managed a 41-yard field goal by Arden Czyzewski, but the Noles struck again before the first period had run its course. A 13-play drive ended with Weldon's eight-yard scoring toss to Amp Lee. When the referee whistled the first period into history, FSU was up 17-3.

But the Gators' offensive brilliance could not be stymied much longer. After a short punt gave UF the ball at the Tribe 37, the visitors narrowed the gap to 17-10 on Matthews' sneak. Every time Florida scored on this December day, the Seminoles lashed back at once. The touchdown that gave Florida State its 24-10 halftime lead came on Edgar Bennett's two-yard run.

The third quarter was still young when Bennett reached paydirt again to cap a 67-yard drive and make the score 31-10. All season long Matthews and the Gators, running out of Spurrier's widely spread-out offensive set, had been able to put points on the board quickly. Down three touchdowns, Shane Matthews moved his men 69 yards in 45 seconds, finishing with a six-point toss to Ernie Mills; the extra point was stuffed by senior Bill Ragans, who was having an outstanding day on defense.

The Florida score brought an FSU score. This 64-yard movement up the field was all Amp Lee. A 36-yard run, which left tacklers in its wake and fans gasping in amazement, set up Lee's 16-yard dash to the end zone and a 38-16 lead. This time Matthews took a little longer to strike back. His previous drive had lasted 45 seconds; this one took 60. In a minute it covered 57 yards, and the quarterback got the t.d. himself on another sneak. Matthews then found tight-end Kirk Kirkpatrick for a two-point conversion, and his team once again trailed by 14.

The ability to strike so quickly might mean a Gator come-back since more than 12 minutes remained. Those Orange and Blue hopes were dashed immediately when Weldon dropped back and found the great Lawrence Dawsey racing down the

UF's Shane Matthews gets set to pass.

east sidelines; Dawsey grabbed the ball and tore 71 yards to the Gator two-yard-line. On the next snap Amp Lee went in, and with 11:56 remaining Florida State had another three-touchdown lead.

Once again Shane Matthews brought the Gators back, but once again it would not be enough. In a seven-play, 68-yard march, the sensational Florida quarterback scored on a nine-yarder to Kirkpatrick. The two-point conversion failed and left the score 45-30. Florida had the ball on two additional occasions as the clock ticked down, but neither time could Matthews' magic reach the end zone.

The post-game wrap-up made it clear that this FSU-UF battle had little to do with defense. The 75 total points were the most ever scored in the series, breaking the 69 in the 1988 game. The Gators had 31 first downs to the Tribe's 19, testimony to the latter's long strikes. Total yards were almost exactly equal, as FSU edged Florida 487 to 484.

The individual numbers revealed that Shane Matthews had thrown 48 times and completed 29 for 351 yards. Ernie Mills, playing his last game in Orange and Blue, grabbed seven

UF's offense, including Ernie Mills (#14), Tre Everett (#24), Kirk Kirkpatrick (#88), and Chris Bromley (#52) listen to quarterback Shane Matthews.

passes for 126 yards. On the other side of the field, Casey Weldon was 13 of 23 for 325 yards. Amp Lee had a career-high 27 rushes for 147 yards. Another item on the post-game stat sheet told an important tale. The category, lost turnovers, read: "Florida-3; Florida State-O."

In 1990, Bobby Bowden's fourth consecutive victory over Florida matched his 1977-1980 run. It also put him one up on Steve Spurrier in this battle between two of the most creative and exciting minds in college football coaching. The fact that the total number of points scored by both teams (75) and by the losing team (30) were the most ever in the UF-FSU series predicted high-scoring offensive displays in the foreseeable future.

1991

The Gators Rise in the Swamp
UF 14 - FSU 9

The two teams facing each other on Florida Field on November 30, 1991, were on different levels emotionally. True, FSU was 10-1 and ranked third in the nation, but they had lost by one point two weeks earlier to their other in-state rival, Miami, and had thus seen their chances for a first-ever national championship die with the infamous "wide right" field-goal attempt. FSU had been ranked No. 1 all season long before that game, after which the 2nd-ranked Miami Hurricanes rose to the top to stay for the rest of the year.

The Gators, No. 5 and 9-1, came into the game on an emotional high. They had posted a 7-0 record against their Southeastern Conference (SEC) foes and cliched their first-ever SEC championship on Nov. 16 when they beat Kentucky.

In a book that was meant to describe the Seminoles' march to the national championship, Ben Brown's *Saint Bobby and the Barbarians* (New York: Doubleday, 1992), the author mentioned that, even before the season had begun, Bowden had considered the UF match-up even more difficult than the Miami game, primarily because of the "ambush atmosphere of raucous Florida Field." The loss to Miami put a heavy burden on Bowden and his assistant coaches.

They had a difficult task of re-invigorating the demoralized team. Not only had the Noles lost their bid for the national championship, but now they were facing a surging Gator squad at the always challenging Florida Field, nicknamed "The Swamp" by coach Spurrier and the fans. UF's only loss was a 38-21 blow-out to Syracuse, a team that FSU had walloped, 46-14, and some might therefore favor the Noles, but the noise factor in The Swamp put visitors at a distinct disadvantage.

UF's Tim Paulk (#99) chases FSU's Casey Weldon (#11).

Going into the game, the two offenses were sizzling and ranked in the top ten in productivity. FSU was averaging 39 points and 460 yards a game, while UF was close behind with nearly 35 points and 470 yards a game. Never before had the two teams met when both were ranked in the top five, and their 19-2 combined record was the best since the series began in 1958. Everyone was expecting a high-scoring free-for-all. What they did not expect was a defensive gem that came down to the final FSU possession.

The UF-FSU game was on the 25th anniversary of the (in)famous Lane Fenner (non)catch, but few fans in the stands probably remembered that. As in that game, this game came down to the final series of plays by FSU in the fourth quarter.

In the end the Gators prevailed 14-9, but it was the defense that sealed the victory. The Gators held the vaunted FSU offense to a field goal and a touchdown. That was even more remarkable when you realize that the Seminoles had a first down at the Florida one-yard-line (from which they scored only a field goal) and another first down at Florida's two-yard-line (from which they scored nothing).

A crowd of 85,461, which was a record for both Florida Field and state, and a national television audience watched as the teams took to the field that hot Saturday afternoon. It came as a surprise to many when the first score did not come until 8:31 of the second period: a Gerry Thomas 19-yard-field goal that gave FSU an early 3-0 lead. The Gators responded with a 10-play, 76-yard touchdown drive that culminated in an Errict Rhett three-yard score that gave the Gators a 7-3 lead.

In the third quarter UF's Shane Matthews rolled out and hit Harrison Houston for a 72-yard strike that put the Gators ahead 14-3. A fourth-quarter drive for the Seminoles culminated in a Weldon-to-Amp Lee pass that scored and cut the Gator lead to 14-9. The Seminoles went for two points, but UF's William Gaines knocked down quarterback Brad Johnson's pass. If the Seminoles had scored the two-point conversion and made it 14-11, a fourth-quarter field goal would have tied it.

UF's Kevin Carter (#57) chases the speedy Terrell Buckley (#27).

In the end it came down to FSU's final play of the game. With 2:11 left in the game, FSU faced a fourth down at the Gators' 14-yard-line. With no time-outs left, Casey Weldon called a pass play. He took the snap, rolled to his right, and looked down field for his receivers. He might have run for a first down, but four quarters of being pounded by the Gator defense had left him exhausted. Instead he winged the ball toward Kez McCorvey, who was sprinting across the middle. Gator Safety Will White tipped it away from McCorvey, but the ball went up into the air. FSU's Matt Frier reached for it, but UF Cornerback Del Speer knocked him away from the ball to preserve the Gator win.

The Seminoles, who had entered the game averaging 205 yards on the ground per game and 4.7 yards a carry, netted only 37 yards and a measly 1.4 average yards that day. Amp Lee had needed only 47 yards to become the fifth Seminole back to rush for a thousands yards in a season, but gained only 24. Florida sacked FSU's quarterback Weldon three times and inflicted

Gator Tony McCoy (#71) and Seminole Johnny Clower (#80) share a few moments after the game.

such a pounding that he needed seven stitches to close a cut on his chin in the first quarter alone.

Errict Rhett rushed for 120 yards that day and became the rushing leader of the SEC year — all on a team known more for its passing than its rushing. UF jumped to 3rd in the polls and was actually mentioned as a dark horse for the national championship, but that was not to be.

UF went on to lose in the Sugar Bowl to Notre Dame, 39-28, and wound up 10-2, ranked seventh in the country. FSU went on to beat Texas A&M 10-2 in the Cotton Bowl and wound up 11-2, ranked fourth in the nation.

The game set several records. FSU's All-American Terrell Buckley had two interceptions and 55 return yards that day to set a NCAA record for career return yards (501) off interceptions (21). The win gave the Gators their first-ever 10-win season.

In his book about Florida's winning of its first SEC title, *Gators* (Orlando: Tribune Publishing, 1992), Coach Spurrier wrote that "This was the most intense, emotional, electrifying game I have ever been involved with as a player or a coach at any level." He attributed much of the emotion to the 75,000 Gator fans who drowned out and gator chomped the 10,000 FSU fans.

In just two short weeks, the Seminoles fell from being No. 1 in the nation to being No. 3 in the state of Florida. "We've gone from being the greatest team in FSU history to being the biggest disappointment in FSU history," said defensive back Errol McCorvey. Coach Bowden added: "Any loss disappoints me. I can't stand them. But I don't know if there's anything else more painful than the last two."

Before the start of the next football season the University of Florida appointed Jeremy Foley as its new athletic director, replacing Bill Arnsparger, who had gone on to coach the San Diego Chargers defense in the National Football League. Foley had begun his UF career with an internship in the Gator Ticket Office in 1976 and had slowly worked his way up to the top. Foley and others helped UF rank among the nation's ten best total athletic programs over the past decade.

1992

The 35th Game Is a Blow-Out
FSU 45 - UF 24

When garnet-and-gold and orange-and-blue gridders ran onto Campbell Stadium turf on November 28, a new dimension was added to the FSU-UF series. The Seminoles' first season in the Atlantic Coast Conference produced the rivalry's first interconference battle: the ACC vs. the SEC.

By game day the peninsular state rivals were both ranked in the AP's top ten: FSU 3rd; UF 6th. Bobby Bowden's Tribe had begun '92 with four consecutive wins over ACC rivals before losing by a field goal in the Orange Bowl to #1-ranked Miami. FSU then won their last four conference games—barely defeating Georgia Tech—before crushing Tulane. By the time the Gators came to town, State was 9-1.

Steve Spurrier's team opened with a victory over Kentucky but then stumbled twice in a row on the road in the SEC. Both Tennessee and Mississippi State soundly defeated the Gators. Standing 1-2, the orange and blue bounced back with six victories over conference foes and a defeat of Southern Miss. Sixth-ranked UF was 8-2 by game day and were champions of the SEC's Eastern Division.

Bowden's 1992 Seminoles were led by three of the nation's most highly publicized college football players. Quarterback Charlie Ward, the basketball team's brilliant point guard, began '92 slowly, throwing first-half interceptions before engineering exciting fourth-quarter victories over Clemson and Tech. By the Florida game, FSU was widely employing the no-huddle shotgun, and Ward and this "Fast Break" offense had become so effective that the QB began to be mentioned in Heisman speculation. Tallahassee freshman Tamarick Vanover produced such sensational kickoff returns, reverses, and pass receptions that he was named freshman player of the year in college football. On defense, Marvin Jones, the greatest linebacker ever to wear the garnet and gold, won both the Butkus and Lombardi awards, finished high in the Heisman vote, and was a consensus All-American.

Spurrier's Gators were led by QB Shane Matthews, also often mentioned in Heisman talk. Matthews, SEC player of the year in '90 and '91, held dozens of school and conference passing marks. Errict Rhett led the UF running game, and on defense linebacker Carlton Miles and defensive back Will White were the standouts.

At kickoff, 68,311 fans, largest crowd ever in newly expanded Campbell Stadium, watched the agile Ward maneuver his squad to a quick 14-0 lead with 9:19 left in the period. A 65-yard drive ended with Sean Jackson's 10-yard run and a 55-yard march saw Ward fire a 7-yarder to Vanover, who crossed the double stripes. Florida came out throwing deep. After several incompletions Matthews connected on a 53-yard heave to

FSU's Corey Fuller intercepts a pass intended for UF's Harrison Houston.

UF's Jack Jackson reaches for a pass behind FSU's Leon Fowler.

Jack Jackson. This play was the key in a march which ended with Shane's 8-yard toss to Aubrey Hill for the score.

The Gators kicked off to the vaunted Vanover, and the freshman responded. Veering to the west sidelines, the Tallahassee Leon prep star raced 80 yards before he was nudged out of bounds. When the UF defense toughened, FSU added a 26-yard Dan Mowery field goal, and at the first quarter gun FSU was ahead 17-7.

Early in the second period the home team got a big break when Derrick Alexander fell on Rhett's fumble at the Gator 39. Eight plays later Tiger McMillon went in from the 2. Mowery's kick put FSU ahead by 17.

The Gators were halted as were the Seminoles, but on fourth down the notoriously weak Florida State kicking game gave the orange and blue a start at the Tribe 46. Matthews struck back. Six plays later his 8-yard pass to tight end Charlie Dean got the touchdown.

After narrowing their deficit to 10, the Gators made a serious mistake. Would they kick off again to Tamarick Vanover?

"We were going to pooch-kick it, but our players convinced me we could cover it," Steve Spurrier said later. Vanover was surprised when the ball headed his way once again. In a post-game interview FSU's #80 said, "They were saying, 'Let's see if he can do it again." And he did: Vanover romped 76 yards to the Gator 24. A key third-down pass from Ward to Kevin Knox set up Ward's 3-yard run into the end zone.

Florida scored next, but the drive, keyed by Matthews' passes to Tre Everett, Willie Jackson and Greg Keller, failed to manage a touchdown. Spurrier had to settle for a 36-yard field goal after the Marvin Jones-led defense stiffened. In the 2:05 left in the half the Ward-Vanover show took the stage again. A 15-yard Vanover reverse, a 15-yard scramble by the elusive Ward, and a 29-yard pass from Charlie to Tamarick reached the 4, where reliable fullback William Floyd got the call and the touchdown. At intermission Florida State led 38-17, and the outcome appeared to be no longer in doubt.

The second half of the 1992 renewal was all anti-climax. Coach Spurrier pulled Matthews and replaced him with Terry

The two sides line up for an FSU play.

Dean. "I thought at that point it was going to be a little difficult for Shane to get enough points to beat FSU," the Gator coach said after the game. He had his mind on saving his QB for the following week's SEC championship game with the Crimson Tide of Alabama. Both teams were a bit sluggish in the 3rd quarter, and the period's only points were put up by the Noles. A 75-yard drive with key passes and runs by Ward ended when Floyd smashed in from the 1 for his second score. The 35th meeting ended with a Terry Dean pass to Willie Jackson to conclude an 80-yard march in the game's closing moments. At the final gun the scoreboard read FSU 45 Florida 24.

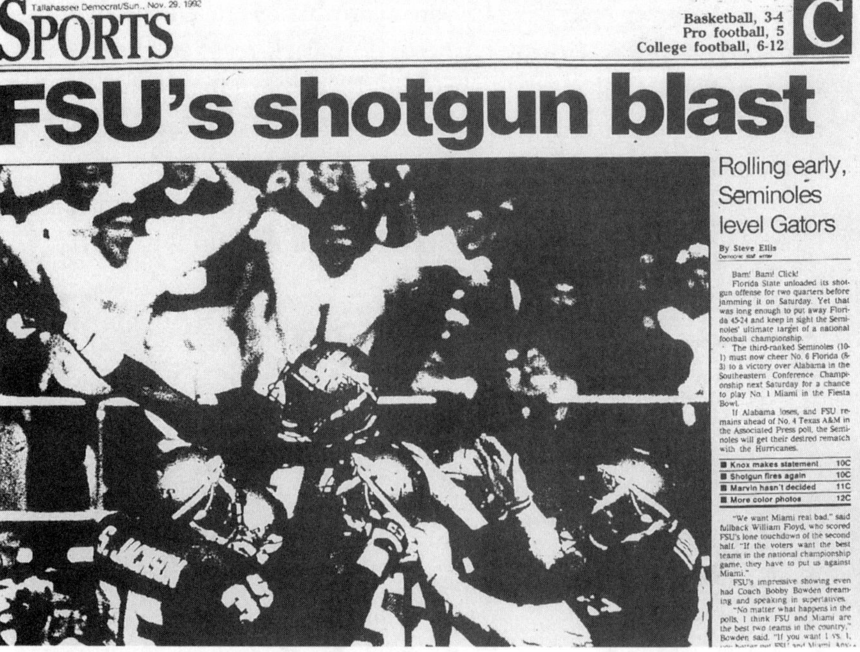
Tallahassee Democrat/Sun., Nov. 29, 1992

SPORTS

Basketball, 3-4
Pro football, 5
College football, 6-12

C

FSU's shotgun blast

Rolling early, Seminoles level Gators

By Steve Ellis
Democrat staff writer

Bam! Bam! Click!

Florida State unloaded its shotgun offense for two quarters before jamming it on Saturday. Yet that was long enough to put away Florida 45-24 and keep in sight the Seminoles' ultimate target of a national football championship.

The third-ranked Seminoles (10-1) must now cheer No. 6 Florida (8-3) to a victory over Alabama in the Southeastern Conference Championship next Saturday for a chance to play No. 1 Miami in the Fiesta Bowl.

If Alabama loses, and FSU remains ahead of No. 4 Texas A&M in the Associated Press poll, the Seminoles will get their desired rematch with the Hurricanes.

■ Knox makes statement 10C
■ Shotgun fires again 10C
■ Marvin hasn't decided 11C
■ More color photos 12C

"We want Miami real bad," said fullback William Floyd, who scored FSU's lone touchdown of the second half. "If the voters want the best teams in the national championship game, they have to put us against Miami."

FSU's impressive showing even had Coach Bobby Bowden dreaming and speaking in superlatives.

"No matter what happens in the polls, I think FSU and Miami are the best two teams in the country," Bowden said. "If you want 1 vs. 1,

Not much post-game analysis was necessary. FSU, in control all the way, edged UF 471 yards to 354 in total offense, but much of Florida's total came with the result already determined. The real show was Ward, Vanover, and a Tribe defense that called a halt when necessary. Charlie got 70 yards on the ground in 9 rushes and completed 27 of 47 for 331 yards in the air. Vanover amassed 239 return, rushing, and reception yards.

The 1992 season for Florida had two games to run. Spurrier's men lost a heartbreaker to 'Bama in the SEC's first playoff and then bounced back to decisively whip N.C. State in the Gator Bowl. The orange and blue wound up ranked 10th by AP.

Bowden's Seminoles, ranked 3rd after the UF victory, went to the Orange Bowl against Big 8 champ Nebraska. On a rainy night in Miami Charlie Ward and Marvin Jones led the garnet and gold to a decisive 27-14 victory. Florida State ended 1992 ranked second in the nation.

Summary of Scores
1958-1992

Year	Winner	Score	Site
1958	UF	21-7	Gainesville
1959	UF	18-8	Gainesville
1960	UF	3-0	Gainesville
1961	—	3-3	Gainesville
1962	UF	20-7	Gainesville
1963	UF	7-0	Gainesville
1964	FSU	16-7	Tallahassee
1965	UF	30-17	Gainesville
1966	UF	22-19	Tallahassee
1967	FSU	21-16	Gainesville
1968	UF	9-3	Tallahassee
1969	UF	21-6	Gainesville
1970	UF	38-27	Tallahassee
1971	UF	17-15	Gainesville
1972	UF	42-13	Tallahassee
1973	UF	49-0	Gainesville
1974	UF	24-14	Tallahassee
1975	UF	34-8	Gainesville
1976	UF	33-26	Tallahassee
1977	FSU	37-9	Gainesville
1978	FSU	38-21	Tallahassee
1979	FSU	27-16	Gainesville
1980	FSU	17-13	Tallahassee
1981	UF	35-3	Gainesville
1982	UF	13-10	Tallahassee
1983	UF	53-14	Gainesville

Year	Winner	Score	Site
1984	UF	27-17	Tallahassee
1985	UF	38-14	Gainesville
1986	UF	17-13	Tallahassee
1987	FSU	28-14	Gainesville
1988	FSU	52-17	Tallahassee
1989	FSU	24-17	Gainesville
1990	FSU	45-30	Tallahassee
1991	UF	14-9	Gainesville
1992	FSU	45-24	Tallahassee

UF wins: 23
FSU wins: 11
Ties: 1

Records from the UF-FSU Series

Most Points by Both Teams: 75 (1990)
Most Points by One Team: 53 by UF (1983)
Most Points by the Losing Team: 30 by UF (1990)
Greatest Point Spread: 49 (1973)
Fewest Points by Both Teams: 3 (1960)

Lettermen of both schools since 1958

UF LETTERMEN

Abbott, Frederic M. 1970,71,72
Abdelnour, Thomas A. 1967,68,69
Ackerman, Brady 1990,91
Adams, Andre E. 1985
Adams, Lawrence H. 1971,74
Adkins, Robert M. 1974,77
Agee, Joseph R., III 1969
Albury, Charles D. 1968,69
Allen, Joseph L. 1973,74,75
Allen, Richard A. 1956,57,59
Allen, William Theo 1982
Alvarez, Carlos 1969,70,71
Amelung, Frank A., Jr. 1967,68,69
Anderson, Anthony L. 1973,74
Anderson, Charlie Neal 1982,83,84,85
Anderson, Eric 1984
Anderson, Jerry D. 1964,65,66
Anderson, Kris H. 1971,72,73
Anderson, Myrick R. 1989,90,91,92
Archie, Pete 1991,92
Arfaras, Nicholas J. 1960,61
Armstrong, Scott W. 1984,85,86
Armstrong, Trace 1988
Ash, Terry D. 1970
Aust, Clifton E. 1971,72,73
Aydt, Timothy E. 1975,76,77
Ayers, William 1957,58
Baeszler, Marquis C. 1964,65,66
Baker, Jay S. 1985
Baldwin, Gregory S. 1988,89
Ball, Clinton R. 1973,74,75
Barber, Terence B. 1988,89,90
Barber, Vernon S. 1973,74,75,76
Barfield, John W. 1965,66,67
Barnard, David 1992
Barnhart, David L. 1968
Barr, Jimmy D. 1969,71
Barrett, Donald James 1964,65,66
Barrow, Gregory John 1980
Bartley, Ephesians 1988,89,90,91
Bartley, Jason 1992
Bartruff, Wm. Owen 1986,87,88
Batten, Thomas E., Jr. 1959,60,61
Beaver, James E. 1959,60,61
Beavin, Paul T. 1987
Beckman, Lars E. 1964,65
Bell, Kerwin D. 1984,85,86,87
Bell, William R. 1977,78
Benjamin, Basil 1986
Bennek, William J. 1977,78
Bennett, Bruce 1963,64,65
Benson, James E., Jr. 1964,65,66
Bernhardt, James T., III 1963,64
Beusse, Carl 1965,66
Bilkie, Chris 1991,92
Billett, Rodney Charles 1982,83,84
Billins, Mike V. 1989
Blair, Steven S. 1975,76,77
Bludworth, David H. 1961
Boardman, Hollis C. 1971,72,73
Boedy, Robert F. 1972,73
Bolduc, Norman 1991
Booth, James K. 1971
Borajkiewicz, Joseph L. 1981
Bowden, David R. 1972,73
Bowen, Hunter S. 1969,70
Bradley, Victor Andrew 1981
Brandon, Michael B. 1989,90,91
Brantley, John W. 1977,78
Brantley, Richard A. 1957,58,59
Brantley, Scot E. 1976,77,78,79
Brewer, Rodney L. 1984,85,86
Brinson, Larry S. 1973,74,75,76
Brodsky, Joseph, Jr. 1978
Bromley, Chris R. 1987,88,89,90
Bromley, Philip Eugene, III 1981,82,83,84
Brooks, Rodney Andrew 1978,80
Brown, Henry J. 1984,85,86,87
Brown, Johnell 1979,80,81,82
Brown, Joseph B. 1964,65

Brown, Lomas 1981,82,83,84
Brown, Merrell R. 1961,62,63
Brown, Mike 1990
Brown, Trell 1977
Brown, Vernell 1982,83,84,85
Brown, Varoly Agusta 1979,80,81,82
Browne, Richard S. 1971,72,73
Buchanan, Richard A. 1969,70,71
Burch, Shannon Leonard 1978,81
Burden, Gregory H. 1984,85
Burdgess, Derrick E. 1977,78
Burnett, Webbie D. 1986,87
Burns, Jack C. 1968,69,70
Butler, Alvin B. 1972,73,74
Butz, Clyde O. 1959
Byers, Bernarr M. 1968
Byrd, Walter O'Neal 1982,84,85,86
Byrge, Earl 1965
Cain, Herbert A. 1976
Cain, John J. 1976
Calhoun, Kelvin 1988
Callahan, Melton V. 1965
Cameron, Glenn S. 1972,73,74
Cameron, Jeff 1982
Campbell, Mark 1992
Cansler, Dale B. 1958, 59
Carey, Craig 1991
Card, Jack D. 1964,65,66
Carpenter, Darrell F. 1973,74,75,76
Carr, Earl 1975,76,77
Carr, William C. 1964,65,66
Carter, Kevin 1991,92
Casey, Charles A. 1964,65
Cash, William K. 1960,61,62
Chandler, Wesley S. 1974,75,76,77
Charlton, Clifford T. 1984, 85,86,87
Cheney, Andrew B. 1969,70
Chorniewy, Thomas F. 1973
Christian, Floyd T., Jr. 1966,67,68
Church, Johnie 1992
Clark, Brian Matthew 1979,80,81
Clark, Carroll H., Jr. 1969,70,71
Clark, Michael Hugh 1978,80
Clark, Randy Charles 1981,82,83
Clark, Ray J. 1987
Clarke, Hagood, III 1961,62,63
Cleveland, Gregory Leon 1982,83,85
Cliett, Gary 1964,65
Clifford, John J. 1970,71,72
Clifford, Thomas A. 1973,74,75
Clifton, William 1962
Cline, James L. 1974,75,76,77
Coburn, Henry K. 1977,78
Cohen, Michel 1991,92
Cole, Dale M. 1987
Cole, John 1964,65,66
Cole, Marshall 1969,70
Coleman, Robert W. 1968,69
Coleman, Ronald L. 1976,78,80
Collins, Chester T., Jr. 1959,60,61
Collins, Juan L. 1977,78
Collinsworth, A. Cris 1977,78,79,80
Colson, Gordon W. 1964,65
Condon, Thomas F. 1971
Conover, William L. 1978
Conrad, Gene G. 1970,71
Cook, Kendall 1992
Coons, John D. 1966,67
Corlew, Reginald R. 1984,85,86,87
Cowans, Alvin J. 1973,74,75,76
Cox, Asa J. 1957,58,59
Crawford, Jeff 1961
Criswell, Ray Allen 1982,83,84,85
Cross, William I. 1976
Crouch, Gantt 1990,91,92
Culpepper, J. Blair 1957,58
Culpepper, J. Broward (Brad) 1988,89,90,91
Culpepper, Philip B. 1960,61,62
Cummings, Rowland 1983,84,85
Curry, Ivory 1980,81,82
Cutfliffe, C. Paige 1965,66
Czyzewski, Arden 1989,90,91
Daniels, Dexter 1992
Daniels, John 1990
Daniels, Tracy D. 1985,87,88
Darby, Alvis R. 1973,74,75
Davidson, Peter B. 1956,57,58
Davis, Calvin Jerome 1980,81
Davis, Henry A. 1974,75
Davis, James M. 1984,85,86,87

Davis, Judd 1992
Davis, Robert S. 1973
Davis, Tony 1992
Dawson, Jeffery T. 1985,86
Day, Jeffrey T. 1988
Deal, Don Lee 1958,59,60
Dean, Charlie 1990,91,92
Dean, George R. 1966,67,68
Dean, Terry 1991,92
Dean, Thomas F. 1960,61
Dee, Steven 1991
Dennis, Guy D. 1966,67,68
Dent, John C. 1961,62,63
Dewitt, Barry G. 1986
Diamond, Gregg 1990,91
Dickens, Gerold Devan 1983,84,85,87
Dickert, Mark 1980
Dickey, Donald B. 1975,76
Didio, Nick 1964,65,66
Dilts, Russell J. 1958,59
Dixon, Cal 1988,89,90,91
Dixon, Dwayne Keith 1980,81,82,83
Dodd, Robert L., Jr. 1960,61
Doddridge, Rock E. 1970
Doel, Duane P. 1970
Dolfi, Thomas N. 1975
Doll, Ronald D. 1972
Donigan, Jimbo 1979
Dorminey, James Dale 1980,83,84
Dorminy, Albert C. 1972
Dorsey, William J. 1966,67,68
Douglas, Donald R. 1989
Dowdy, William E. 1969,70,71
Downs, Bobby C. 1966,67
Downie, Charles V. (Pepper) 1982,83,84
Drew, Douglas Edward 1980,81,82,83
DuBose, Jimmy D. 1973,74,75
Duhart, Thomas 1984,85
Duncan, Monty 1990,91,92
Dunn, E. McAuley, Jr. 1961
Dunn, James H. 1956,57,58
Dunn, Henry H., Jr. 1969
Dupree, Lawrence W. 1962,63,64
Dupree, Michael D. 1976,77,78
Durden, John P. 1988,89
Durrance, Thomas L. 1969,70,71
Duven, Gary G. 1966,67,68
Easmon, Willie Chas. (Ricky)
1981,82,83,84
Eastman, Ward T. 1973
Eckdahl, Jack L. 1967,68,69
Edge, Shayne 1991,92
Edgington, Dan T. 1957,58,59
Edmiston, Bart 1992
Ellenburg, James S. 1958,59
Ellis, Brent C. 1987,88,89,90
Ellis, Gary Richard 1982,83,84
Ellison, Melvin Alan 1982,83,84
Ely, Mark M. 1967,68,69
Ely, Stephen 1968
Enclade, Ronald 1974,75,76,78
Entzminger, Wade D. 1961
Everett, Tre 1990,91,92
Ewaldsen, Paul H. 1965,66,67
Ewell, Cecil D., Jr. 1960,61
Ewing, Steven R. 1986,87
Fain, Richard A. 1987,88,89
Faix, John W. 1968,70,71
Fannin, David E. 1958,59
Farmer, Henry B., Jr. 1961,62
Faulkner, Christopher 1979,80,81,82
Feiber, John K. 1964,65
Ferdinand, Leser 1992
Ferguson, Dwayne M. 1986
Field, Michael S. 1970
Fields, Wayne G. 1972,73,74,75
Fike, Dan C., Jr. 1979,80,81,82
Fiorillo, William S. 1978
Fisher, Brian 1992
Fisher, James D. 1974,75,76
Fisher, Robin Lynn 1979,80,81
Fleming, Don 1956,57,58
Fleming, Dennis W. 1976
Flournoy, Melvin A. 1976,77
Floyd, John P. 1974
Foldberg, Henry C. 1971,72,73
Forrester, David D. 1975,76,77
Forrester, Dennis D. 1975,76,77
Foster, R.E. III 1968
Fox, Brian 1990,91

Francis, John David 1985,86,88,89
Franco, Richard J. 1969,70,71
Franklin, Jim 1991
Fraser, Ryan Taylor 1980,81,82
Frazier, Daryl 1992
Frazier, Edward E. 1987
Freeman, Kevin 1991,92
Fromang, Vernon B. 1976
Fuller, William L. 1970,71
Gaffney, Derrick T. 1975,76,77
Gaffney, Donald G. 1973,74,75
Gaffney, Johnny Anthony 1980
Gaffney, Warren B. 1975,76,78
Gagner, Larry 1963,64,65
Gailey, Chan 1971,72,73
Gaines, William 1990,91
Gainey, James Preston 1981,82
Gaisford, William J. 1967,68
Gallon, Russell Alvin 1981,82
Galloway, David Lawrence 1977,79,80,81
Galloway, Harold 1978
Garcia, Pete 1980
Garland, Samuel Albert 1983,84,85
Garrett, Curtis Lamar 1980
Gatlin, S. Todd 1984,86,87,88
Geiger, Carey H. 1971,72,73
George, Leonard 1970,71,72
George, Leroy Joseph 1985
Getzen, James G. 1970
Gerzina, Jack Robert 1983,84,85
G'Fransisco, Mark Anthony 1983
Ghesquiere, G.D., Jr. 1967,68,69
Giannamore, Lawrin F. 1957,58,59
Gilbert, Lewis H., Jr. 1975,76,77
Giles, Donald R. 1958
Gill, Charles W., Jr. 1960
Gilliam, Fendrid (Sonny) 1979,80,81,83
Gilmore, Michael 1991,92
Giordano, Donald M. 1965,66,67
Glenn, Kevin 1991
Glenn, Thomas E. 1967
Glover, Dwayne M. 1985,86,87
Golden, Dean 1991,92
Golden, Timothy George 1980
Good, Joseph Earl 1983
Good, Tim 1972
Goodman, Donald E. 1959,60,61
Gordon, Raji B. 1987
Gould, Octavius D. 1986
Gowland, Jan E. 1970,71,72
Gramling, Donnie L. 1968
Grandison, Greg D. 1989
Grandy, Stuart G. 1964,65,66
Graves, Homer E. 1958,59
Grebe, Daniel E. 1976
Green, Bobby Joe 1958,59
Green, Napoleon, Jr. 1976,77
Green, Reggie 1992
Green, Samuel L. 1972,73,74,75
Green, Tony E. 1974,75,76,77
Gregory, Thomas R. 1960,61
Grieves, Chris 1979
Griffin, James 1962
Griffin, Skil 1964
Griffeth, James K., Jr. 1975
Griffith, Clinton D., Jr. 1972,73,74
Griffith, Todd W., Jr. 1967,68,69
Groves, Cecil Timothy 1978,79,80
Grow, Monty R. 1989,92
Guido, Michael F. 1977
Gunter, William B. 1971
Gunter, William J. 1989,91,92
Gurkin, Van M. 1970
Hackney, Robert R. 1972
Hadley, James F. 1967,68
Hager, Teddy C. 1968,69,70
Hall, James E., Jr. 1962,63,64
Hampton, Lorenzo Timothy 1981,82,83,84
Hanks, Ben 1992
Hansberry, William 1969
Harlow, Joseph G. 1970,72
Harper, Jack R. 1964,65,66
Harrell, James C. 1977,78
Harrell, Robert S. 1969,70,71
Harris, Roy Elliott 1981,82,83
Haston, Henry 1991,92
Hatch, Charles E. 1976,77,78
Hatch, Lawrence 1991,92
Hatcher, Edmund (Brad) 1988,89

Hawkins, Robert A. 1958,59
Healey, Michael J. 1967,68
Heckman, Velles A. 1956,57,58
Heidt, William S. 1964,65,66
Helton, Charles K. 1967,68,69
Henderson, Joseph 1983
Hergert, Joseph M. 1956,57,58
Hewko, Alex Robert 1980
Hewko, Eric 1976
Hewko, Robert Todd 1980,81,82
Hickenlooper, Walter A. 1960,61,62
Hicks, Louis E. 1961
Higgs, Earl 1992
Hill, Aubrey 1991,92
Hinson, William Dewayne 1982,83,84
Hinton, Dozyier 1976,78
Hiott, George Earl 1985
Hipp, Brian 1968
Hitchcock, David P. 1971,72,73
Hodges, Eric N. 1985,86
Hoffman, Robert H. 1985
Holland, Walter S. 1960,61,62
Hontas, Mark J. 1972
Hood, Charles H. 1970
Hood, William K. 1958,59,60
Hoover, Robert R. 1960,61,62
Hosack, Robert L. 1961,62
Hough, Wallace Oliver, Jr. 1980
Houston, Harrison 1990,91,92
Hoye, Francis O. 1965
Hudson, William D. 1957,58,59
Hungerbuhler, Tom J. 1966,67
Hunt, John Stephen 1981,82,83
Hurbanis, Matt 1991,92
Hurm, Mark 1981,82,83
Hutcherson, Dale L. 1969,70,71
Hutchinson, Scott R. 1974,75,76,77
Iannarelli, Ronald J. 1972
Infante, Gelindo 1960,61,62
Ismail, Hesham 1988,89,90,91
Jackson, Fernando C. 1980,81,82
Jackson, Jack 1992
Jackson, R.B. 1964,65
Jackson, Spencer 1979,80,81,82
Jackson, Terrell 1990,91
Jackson, Willie B. 1970,71,72
Jackson, Willie, Jr. 1991,92
Jacobsen, Edward P. 1977
James, John W., Jr. 1970,71
James, Vernon L. 1976,77,78
Jetter, Brian L. 1965,66,67
Johnson, Alonzo 1981,83,84,85
Johnson, David J. 1977,78
Johnson, E. Julian, Jr. 1965
Johnson, Ellis 1991,92
Johnson, James W. 1978
Johnson, Philip J. 1989
Johnson, Thomas W. 1989
Jones, Alton Marcus 1981,82
Jones, Anthony D. (Tony) 1986,87,88,89
Jones, C. Jerome 1961,62,63
Jones, Eugene Van 1979,81
Jones, Jackie D. 1959
Jones, James L. 1985
Jones, James R. 1979,80,81,82
Jones, Leroy 1991,92
Jones, Richard E., III 1961,62
Jones, Roger D. 1977,78
Jones, Rodney U. 1984,85,86
Jones, Vince 1979,82,83
Jordan, Jimmy A. 1964
Kalamaras, Jimmy S. 1979,80,81,82
Kanter, Jeffrey D. 1975,76,77
Katz, Jack 1962,63,64
Keefe, Lawrence 1981,82
Keller, Greg A. 1989,90,92
Kelley, James M. 1968,69,70
Kelley, Tommy R. 1960,61,62
Kellom, Douglas Lee 1980
Kelly, William J. 1970
Kendrick, Preston 1972,73,74
Kendrick, Vincent 1971,72,73
Kennedy, Jeremy 1992
Kennedy, Larry 1991,92
Kennell, Thomas H. 1969
Kensler, Richard B. 1970,71
Ker, Crawford Francis 1983,84
Kerr, Mike A. 1989
Kiefer, Steven R. 1976

Kiley, James M. 1968,69
Killer, Clyde 1964
King, Mark 1971
King, Sylvester 1975,76,77
Kirk, Dick 1963,64,65
Kirkpatrick, Kirk 1987,88,89,90
Kirkpatrick, Wesley 1961
Kissenberth, Andy 1992
Knapp, Donald O. 1964,65,66
Knight, Ricky S. 1984,85
Knight, William Kyle 1980,81,82
Knight, Riley J. 1984
Kochevar, Matthew 1992
Korff, Mark C. 1983,84
Kreis, James D. 1977,78
Kruse, Kim P. 1973
Kurzu, Robert Wayne 1981,83
Kynes, James H. 1972,73,74
Kynes, William L. 1975,76
Lacer, John B. 1971,72,73
Laczko, Kevin 1990
Lager, Willie 1962,63
Lake, Eddie 1992
Lamb, Doug 1966
Lamberth, Jason G. 1986,87
Landry, John Adelard 1982
Lang, Broughton Keith 1981,82,83
Lang, William James 1986,87,88
Langelier, Kirby 1991
LaPete, Frank L. 1974,75
Lasky, Francis J. 1962,63
Lasky, Robert F. 1986
Lawless, Richard B. 1972,73,74
Lawrence, Raymond Eugene, Jr. 1980
Lay, Kris 1991
LeCount, Terry 1975,76,77
Lee, William L., Jr. 1969
Lemon, Samuel 1976
Lenard, Gary W. 1976,77
Lennon, Steve M. 1985
Leon, Anthony Thomas 1988
Lescano, Pepe J. 1987
Libertore, L.P., Jr. 1960,61,62
Lily, Robert Anthony 1980,81,82,83
Little, David Lamar 1977,78,79,80
Lockett, Thomas E. 1984,85
Loden, Steve P. 1986,87
Logan, Kevin R. 1974,75
Loper, Gerald C. 1973,74,75
Lomack, Tony 1986,87,88,89
Lucas, Leonard LaVann 1971
Lucey, Don T. 1958,59
Luckie, Dock 1980
Luczko, George 1975
Lyle, Robert T., Jr. 1962,63,64
MacBeth, Jon L. 1958,59,60
Mack, Sam H. 1961
Mack, Stephon 1989,90
MacLean, Sydney W. 1962,63,64
MacInness, Henry A. 1984
Maggio, Philip J. 1965,66
Mahood, Jack 1965,66
Maliska, Paul W. 1967,68,69
Maloy, Bruce L. 1985
Malone, Kedra 1990,92
Mallory, LeRoy T. 1971
Mangus, George 1991
Mann, Thomas D. 1967,68
Manry, Daniel S., Jr. 1965
Marshall, Scott R. 1981,82,83
Marshall, Wilbur B. 1980,81,82,83
Massey, James Dorsey 1983,84,86,87
Matthews, Lynn 1964,65
Matthews, Preston 1966
Matthews, Shane 1990,91,92
Maynor, James M. 1974,75,76
McAndrew, James B. 1986,87
McBride, William A. 1968
McCall, Wayne C. 1964,66,67
McCallister, Frederick M. 1980,81,82,83
McCann, George H. 1966,67
McCarron, Pat 1965,66
McCarthy, Frank Allen 1982,84,85,86
McClendon, Willie A. 1988,89,90,91
McCoun, Joseph C. 1971,72,73
McCoy, Tony B. 1987,88,91
McCravy, Daniel W. 1971
McDonald, Raymondo 1982,83,84,85
McGinty, Robert F. 1986,87
McGrady, Willie J. 1987,88

McGriff, Lee C. 1972,73,74
McGriff, Mark C. 1986,87,88
McGriff, Perry C., Jr. 1958,59
McIntosh, David 1967
McKeel, Frederick G. 19864,66,67
McKeever, Juan Devito 1980,81,82,83
McLellan, Jason 1988
McMillan, R. Wendell 1970
McMillian, Henry 1992
McNabb, Dexter E. 1988,89,90,91
McTague, Joseph 1982
McTheny, Guy C. 1967,68,69
Meyers, Glenn S. 1981
Mickell, Darren 1990,91
Midden, Mark B. 1977,78
Milby, Robert V. 1958,59
Miles, Carlton 1989,90,91,92
Miller, Leon Patrick 1982,83,84,85
Miller, Steve 1981
Mills, Ernie L. 1987,88,89,90
Miranda, Victor R. 1957,58,60
Mitz, Alonzo L. 1982,83,84,85
Monk, Harold 1991,92
Montgomery, Brian 1990
Moore, Eddy L. 1970,71,73
Moore, Michael L. 1971,72,73
Moore, Nathaniel 1972,73
Moore, Robert L. 1974,75,76
Moorer, Patrick J. 1986,87,88,89
Morgan, Jimmy S. 1962,63
Morgan, Robert E., II 1974,75,76
Morrail, Matthew 1977,78,79
Morris, John 1964
Morris, Kyle S. 1988,90
Morris, R. Larry 1970,72
Morris, Terry E. 1966,67,68
Morrison, Sherwood C. 1972,73,74
Moten, Ronald Edwin 1982,84,85,86
Moyle, Jon Cameron 1980,81,82,83
Mularkey, Michael R. 1980,81,82
Mulberry, Ricky L. 1984,85,86,87
Mulliniks, Bruce A. 1974,75,76
Murphy, Alvin D. 1962,63,64
Murray, Mark A. 1987,88,89,90
Myles, Godfrey C. 1988,89,90
Nalls, Ronnie 1961,62
Nadone, David Michael 1983,84
Nattiel, Ricky R. 1983,84,85,86
Neal, Frankie Leon 1983,84,85
Neely, Glenn M. 1987,88,89,90
Nelson, William John 1983,84
Newbern, William A. 1956,57,58
Newcomer, Gerald C. 1962,63,64
Newman, Andy 1987,90
Newman, Mark L. 1976
Newton, Timothy Reginald 1981,82,83,84
Nichols, Johnny R. 1988,89,90,91
Nicoletto, Joseph B. 1985,86,87,88
Norris, Kenneth L. 1959,60
Norwood, David Anthony 1980
Nugent, William S. 1972,73
Ochab, Larry 1979,80
Odom, Gerald S. 1960,62,63
Odom, Gerald S., Jr. 1987,88,89,90
Odom, Jason 1992
Odom, Walter Amos 1983,84,87
O'Donnell, James D. 1961,62,63
Oliva, John E. 1961
Oliver, Louis 1985,86,87,88
Oliver, Marquette D. 1989,90,91,92
Ortega, Ralph 1972,73,74
Padgett, Aubrey G., Jr. 1972,73
Page, Edward E. 1959,60
Palahach, Michael 1969
Palmer, Sorola 1992
Pappas, Geoff T. 1988
Parham, Duncan A. 1984
Parker, Joseph L. 1971,72,73
Parker, Paul P. 1972,73
Parrish, Alvin L. 1975,76
Partin, Walter D. 1958,59,60
Pasteris, Joseph D. 1966,67
Patchen, Patrick N. 1958,59,60
Patrick, Lawrence H. 1980,81,82
Paulk, Tim 1988,89,90,91
Paulson, Gunnar F. 1969
Peace, Wayne Lamar 1980,81,82,83
Peacock, Harold E. 1968
Pearson, James F. 1961,62,63
Pearson, Matt 1992

Peddie, Thomas Monroe 1983,84,85
Peek, David H. 1970,71
Peek, Eugene G. 1967,68
Peek, Scott I., Jr. 1977
Pennington, Leon Tyrone 1982,83,84,85
Perez, Ron 1992
Perkins, Chris Edwards 1983,84
Perry, Darryl L. 1989
Perry, Herbert E. 1987,88
Peters, Anton B., Jr. 1961,62
Petersen, Gary L. 1970,71
Pettee, Roger 1962,63,64
Pharr, Philip 1978,79,80
Phillips, James C. 1978
Pilcher, Ray C., Jr. 1970,71
Pinner, Patrick E. 1985,86,87
Pippin, Charles 1966
Pleasants, Gordon 1979,80
Plonk, Daniel Warren 1979,80,81,82
Poe, Alan 1964,65
Poff, William D. 1970,71,72
Portale, Joseph J. 1976,77,78
Posey, David E. 1973,74,75,76
Pouncy, Carlton 1991
Powell, Brad 1968,69,70
Powell, Phil 1979
Pracek, Robert L. 1959
Pratt, James Philip 1982
Pratt, Ralph C., Jr. 1976,78
Preston, John H. 1964,65,66
Prioleau, Carl Walker 1979,80
Pupello, Joseph C. 1974,75,76
Pursell, Ron 1964,65
Randolph, Kelvin 1990,91,92
Raymond, Robert John 1983,84
Reaves, Thomas J. 1969,70,71
Rebol, Richard 1968,69
Redmond, John J. 1979,80,81,82
Register, Michael A. 1986
Rentz, Ralph L. 1966,67,68
Reuter, Jeff S. 1987,88
Revels, James C., III 1971,72,73
Reynolds, Clifton 1986,87,88
Reynolds, Joseph R. 1975
Reynolds, Ted 1991
Rhett, Errict 1990,91,92
Rhyne, James R. 1958,59
Rich, Michael L. 1969,70,71
Richards, James T. 1973,74,75
Richardson, Huey L. 1987,88,89,90
Richbourg, William B. 1962,63,64
Ricketts, Mike 1979,80
Riggins, Anthony 1992
Ringgold, Donald W. 1960,61
Rittgers, Rex Von 1966
Roberts, Charles A. 1956,57,58
Robinson, Ed 1990,91,92
Robinson, John L. 1987
Robinson, Rocky 1970
Robinson, Tony L. 1977,78
Rolle, Garrison Anthony 1982,83,84
Rone, George H. (Hank) 1989
Roth, Jeffery Neil 1985,86,87,88
Rowell, Tony D. 1988,89,90,91
Royal, Robert D., Jr. 1958,59,60
Ruland, Ryan 1990,91,92
Russell, Kenneth W. 1962,63,64
Rushing, George 1991,92
Ruth, Richard E. 1976,77
Santille, D. Michael 1966
Scavella, Sam P. 1989,91
Schanbacher, Stephen F. 1977
Schmidt, Carl F. 1970
Schnebly, John M. 1969,70,71
Schroeder, Douglas W. 1976,77,78
Schulet, Scott A. 1975,76
Schultheis, Arthur L., Jr. 1980,81,82,83
Schultz, Fred W. 1956,58
Scott, John L. 1985
Seager, Mark A. 1987
Seal, Howard K. 1974
Seals, Roger K. 1959,60
Senterfitt, Donald R. 1959,60
Sever, Tyson L. 1972,73,74
Sever, William G. 1973,74
Seymour, Harold D. 1964,65
Shannon, Thomas J., Jr. 1962,63,64
Sheer, Thomas L. 1956,57,58
Sheppard, Joseph E. 1971,72
Sibbald, Roger Dwayne 1980,82,83,84

Silman, John S. 1970
Sills, Kevin W. 1985,87,88
Simmons, Stacey A. 1986,87,88
Sims, Robert B. 1986,87
Sinardi, Nick J. 1969
Skalaski, Charles W., III 1976,77
Skelly, Richard J. 1960
Skrivanek, Britt E. 1967,68,69
Slack, Arthur R. 1958,59,60
Smith, Andrew Walter 1981
Smith, Cedric D. 1986,87,88,89
Smith, Dexter A. 1989,90,91,92
Smith, Douglas Earl 1980,82
Smith, Emmitt J. 1987,88,89
Smith, Johnny Wayne 1980
Smith, Lex 1989,91,92
Smith, Linzey T. 1984
Smith, Michael B. 1973,74,75
Smith, Thomas R., Jr. 1959,60,61
Smith, W. Lawrence 1966,67,68
Smojver, Walter (Wally) 1980
Snead, Willis L. 1987,88
Snead, Neal 1964,65
Sorenson, Douglas 1969,70,71
Speer, Del A. 1989,90,91,92
Speer, James H. 1987,88,89,90
Spencer, James A. (Jimmy) 1988,89,90
Spierto, John M. 1986,87,88
Splane, T. Douglas 1965,66,67
Spurrier, Stephen O. 1964,65,66
(Heisman Trophy)
Stacy, Curtis Dale 1982,83,84,85
Stanfield, Michael D. 1972,73,74
Stanley, Reggie 1989
Staples, Russell F. 1961,62
Starkey, David B. 1972,73
Starling, Bruce C. 1960,61
Starowesky, Richard K. 1987,88,89
Steen, Malcolm E. 1967,68,69
Stephens, G.H. 1960
Stephens, Jimmy Ray 1973,75,76
Stephens, Robert L. 1971
Stephens, Tony R. 1976,77,78
Stephenson, George K. 1966
Stipe, Steven D. 1984,85,86
Stoner, Ronald E. 1961
Storey, Matt 1979
Subers, James Innes 1978,79,80
Sullivan, Alonzo L. 1988,89,90,91
Sullivan, George T. 1975
Summers, Jacob A. 1972,73,74
Sutton, Yancey M. 1978,79,80
Swafford, Donald L. 1976,77,78
Swain, David 1991,92
Swanz, Robert J. 1975,76,77
Taggert, George E. 1970
Talbot, Randy W. 1972,73,74
Tannen, Steven O. 1967,68,69
Tanner, Clarke 1992
Taotoai, Ioasa (Josh) 1989
Taylor, Ryan 1990,91,92
Teeler, Dan B. 1987
Tennell, Gregory L.V. 1975,77
Thomas, Gary 1963,64,65
Thomas, Harvey L. 1988,89,91,92
Thompson, Jack B., III 1961,62,63
Thompson, John C. 1960
Thompson, Tim E. 1974
Tinny, Donald Frederick 1983,84,85
Tolliver, Collie, Jr. 1981
Totten, Mark A. 1975,76,77
Trammell, Allen R., Jr. 1964,65
Trapp, Richard E. 1965,66,67
Travis, Larry L. 1960,61,62
Tribble, Keith R. 1974,75,76
Trimble, Barnard Scott 1982,83,84
Trueheart, Harold S., Jr. 1961,62
Tucker, John 1964
Turman, Lloyd A. 1967,68
Uspensky, Michael N. 1969
Van Wie, Donnie 1979
Vargecko, Paul J. 1959,60,61
Vaughan, Bruce Allen 1980,81,82,83
Vaughn, Lane W. 1974
Vinesett, Jerry D. 1968,69,70
Voor, Joseph B. 1978
Vorwerk, Joseph G. 1986,87
Wabbersen, Chuck 1989,90
Wages, Harmon L. 1966,67
Walker, Barry S. 1977,78

Walker, Garry L. 1968,69,70
Warbritton, William R. 1970
Warner, Edwin R. 1966
Waters, Anthony N. 1977,78
Watkins, Kerry 1986,87,88,89
Watson, Jim 1990,91,92
Waxman, Mike 1964,65
Wehking, Robert J. 1959,60,61
Welch, James J. 1969
Westbrook, Jack E. 1958,59
Weston, Rhondy 1985,86,87,88
Whatley, John 1964,65
White, Adrian D. 1984,85,86
White, Arthur 1984,85,86
White, Brian 1992
White, Curtis 1988
White, Mark V. 1988,89,90,91
White, Paul E. 1959,60,61
White, Will D. 1989,90,91,92
Whited, Rod 1991,92
Whittaker, John Lee 1980,82
Wickline, Gregory Joe 1980
Wiechmann, Bret N. 1983,84,85,86
Weigmann, Thomas John 1980,81,82
Wiggins, Lloyd G. 1970
Wilder, Willie B. 1975,76,77
Wildman, Charles F. 1973,75
Williams, Alan K. 1976,77
Williams, Anthony C. 1984,85,86,87
Williams, Burton C. 1964,65
Williams, Charles 1974,75,76,77
Williams, Daniel M. 1969,70
Williams, David W. 1985,86,87,88
Williams, Derald L. 1980
Williams, Donald E. 1968,69,70
Williams, Hal 1986
Williams, Jarvis E. 1984,85,86,87
Williams, John D. 1972,73,75
Williams, John D. 1990
Williams, John L. 1982,83,84,85
Williams, Keith Carnell 1982,84,85,86
Williams, R.L. (Ricky) 1981,82,83,84
Williams, Roderic M. 1973,74,75
Williams, Terry Claitte 1980
Williams, Wayne D. 1985,86,87,88
Williamson, Kendrick W. 1957,58,59
Williamson, Larry C. 1969
Windham, Joseph N. 1954,57,58
Winters, Alex P. 1975
Wood, G.P. 1961
Woulard, Darrell B. 1986,87
Wright, Charlie 1986,87,88
Wright, David A. 1975,76,77
Wunderly, Joseph A. 1973,74
Yancey, James M. 1969,70,71
Yarbrough, James 1966,67,68
Young, James W. 1959,60,61
Young, Kurt B. 1988,90
Young, Tyrone D. 1979,80,81,82
Youngblood, Herbert J. 1968,69,70
Yepremian, Berj S. 1977,78
Zimmerman, Jeffrey Alan
1983,84,85,86
Zukley, Jack E. 1975,77

FSU LETTERMEN

Abbott, Bryce 1989,90,91
Abraham, Clifton 1991,92
Abraira, Philip 1967,68,69
Adams, Kevin 1991
Adams, Robert 1978,80
Alexander, Derrick 1992
Alexander, Ken 1990,91,92
Allen, Billy 1981,82,83,84
Allen, Clyde 1990,91,92
Allen, Greg 1981,82,83,84
Allen, Mike 1972,73,74
Allen, Steve 1990,91
Alvarez, David 1990
Amman, Richard 1969,70,71
Anderson, Bob 1973
Anderson, Bobby 1971,72,73
Andrews, Paul 1959,60,61
Andrews, Richie 1987,88,89,90
Anthony, Terry 1986,87,88,89
Armella, Enzo 1992
Arnold, Phil 1971,72,73
Ashley, Tracy 1981,82,83
Ashmore, Robert 1969,70,71
Askin, Ahmet 1972,73
Avezzano, Joe 1963,64,65
Baggett, Leo 1954,55,56,58
Bagnell, Clare (Bud) 1956,57,58,59
Bailey, Tom 1968,69,70
Bailey, Winfred 1962,63,64
Baker, Bill 1957,58
Baker, Robbie 1989,90,91,92
Baker, Shannon 1989,90,91,92
Barco, Barry 1983,84,85
Barnes, Mike 1976,77
Barr, Mike 1990,92
Barwick, Parrish 1982,84,85,86
Bass, Theron 1968,69,70
Bassett, DAvid 1988,89,90
Battaglia, Carmen 1955,56,57,58
Beckman, Ed 1973,74,75,76
Bell, Bruce 1973
Bengston, Brian 1970
Bennett, Edgar 1987,89,90,91
Benson, Joe 1966,67,68
Berry, Louis 1983,84,85,86
Beville, Steve 1969
Bibent, Maury 1963,64,65
Bickford, Roy 1959,60,61
Bigbie, Abner 1958,59,60
Biletnikoff, Fred 1962,63,64
Black, Jimmy 1973,74,76
Blankenship, Buddy 1965
Blatt, Mike 1965,66,67
Blazovich, Mike 1960,61,62
Bloodworth, Steve 1983
Bonasorte, Monk 1977,78,79, 80
Bowden, Jeff 1981,82
Braggins, David 1965,66
Brannon, Tom 1979,80,81
Bratton, Steve 1970,71,72,73
Bright, Leon 1974,75,76
Brinkley, Larry 1961,62,63
Brooks, Derrick 1991,92
Brown, Bill 1955,56,57,58
Brown, John 1986,87,89
Brown, Lavon 1989,90,91,92
Brown, Mack 1972,73
Brownlee, Roger 1981,82
Bruner, Jerry 1961,62,63
Bryant, Philip 1985
Buckley, Terrell 1989,90,91
Bugar, Mike 1965,67,68
Burkhardt, Bill 1966
Burnett, Ken 1980,81,82
Burt, Bobby 1968
Burton, Clint 1966,67,68
Bush, Devin 1992
Butler, Bobby 1977,78,79,80
Butler, LeRoy 1987,88,89
Butts, Marion 1987,88
Cahoon, Phil 1973,74
Calhoun, Charles 1961,62,63
Campbell, Allen Dale 1981,82
Campbell, Bill 1965,66
Campbell, Danny 1992
Camps, Joe 1974,75,76

Capece, Bill 1977,78,79,80
Cappelen, Davy 1976,77,78,79
Cappleman, Bill 1968,69
Carballo, Manny 1982
Carolla, Phil 1986,87,88
Carreker, Alphonso 1980,81,82,83
Carrell, Duane 1969,70,71
Carruthers, Kirk 1989,90,91
Carter, Aaron 1974,75,76,77
Carter, Dexter 1986,87,88,89
Carter, Keith 1986,87,88,89
Carter, Pat 1984,85,86,87
Carter, Walter 1976,77,78,79
Causey, Jim 1962,63
Caven, Jay 1976,77
Chaney, James 1988,89,90,91
Chavers, Lenny 1981,83,84,85
Cherry, Gator 1976,77
Cheshire, Bill 1967,68
Childers, Sam 1978,79,80,81
Cicalese, Pat 1984
Clark, Deondri 1989,90,91,92
Clark, Ed 1985
Clark, Ed 1989,90,92
Clayton, Harvey 1980,81,82
Clower, Johnny 1989,90,91
Coes, Richard 1990,91,92
Coffield, Randy 1973,74,75
Coggin, Redus 1980,81,82
Coker, Kirk 1984,85
Coleman, Jerry 1981,82
Collier, Danny 1980
Cone, Kent 1959,60
Conoly, Forrest 1992
Conway, Pat 1964,65,66
Cooper, Burt 1972,73,74
Coppess, Ron 1974
Corcoran, Dan 1976
Corlew, Tim 1988
Corral, Kent 1970,71
Coursey, Jarvis 1978,79,80,81
Cowart, Chris 1991,92
Cox, Billy 1966,67,68
Craig, John 1954,55,57,58
Crockett, Zack 1992
Crowe, Andy 1992
Crowe, John 1966,67,68
Curchin, Jeff 1968,69
D'Alessandro, George 1964,64,65
Daly, Bill 1961,62,63
Dane, Doug 1975,76,77
Daniel, Jim 1959,60,61
Daniels, Dan 1971
Darsey, Bruce 1960,61,62
Davis, Bo 1958
Davis, Bob 1983
Davis, Brian 1985,86,88
Davis, Darish 1981,82
Davis, Ed 1971,72,73
Davis, George 1969
Davison, Mike 1972,73,74
Dawsey, Lawrence 1987,88,89,90
Dawson, Bill 1962,63,64
Dawson, Rhett 1969,70,71
Dees, Allen 1970,71,72
DeFrancesco, Frank 1960,61
Dely, Aaron 1992
DeMaria, John Jr. 1970,71,72,73
Denson, Dwayne 1984
Deremer, Jeff 1990,91
Dillaberry, Jason 1990
DiMare, Scott 1986,88
Dinkins, Howard 1988,89,90,91
Dixon, Reggie 1989,90,91
Dodge, Dedrick 1986,87,88,89
Donaldson, John 1992
Donatelli, Donald 1959,60,61
Dowell, J.D. 1983,84
Downey, Joe 1972,73,74
Dukes, Jamie 1982,83,84,85
Duley, Bill 1975,76,77
Eaford, John 1984,86
Eagerton, Terry 1967,68
Eason, Chuck 1966,67,68
Edwards, Jack 1962,63,64
Ehler, Howard 1963,64,65
Ekonomou, Nick 1988,89
El Shahawy, Magdi 1987,88
Elam, Bobby 1972,73
Elliot, Chuck 1966,67,68

Ellison, 'O Mar 1992
Espenship, Jack 1958,59
Everett, Jimmy 1972,73,74,75
Falvo, Tony 1974,75
Feely, Eddie 1960,61,62
Felder, Kenny 1990,91
Fenner, Lane 1966,67
Fenwick, Jack 1966,67,68
Ferguson, Charles 1978
Ferguson, Chip 1985,86,87,88
Ferguson, Matt 1990
Ferrell, Marvin 1990,92
Fick, Happy 1960
Fillyaw, Terry 1991
Fiore, Dano 1971
Flasher, Tim 1984
Flath, John 1990,91,92
Flowers, Jackie 1976,77,78,79
Floyd, Don 1962,63,64
Floyd, Victor 1985,86,87,88
Floyd, William 1991,92
Fontes, Frank 1970,71
Footman, Dan 1991,92
Fotjik, Brad 1982,83
Fountain, Bob 1956,57,58
Fowler, Leon 1987,88,89,90
Freeman, Corian 1989,90,91,92
Frier, Matt 1990,91,92
Fucarino, Dan 1975
Futch, Garry 1979,80,81
Futch, Greg 1977,78,79,80
Gabbard, Steve 1985,86,87,88
Gainer, Herb 1984,85,86,87
Galloway, Ed 1992
Gardner, Jeff 1973,74,75
Garvin, Terry 1964,65
Gavin, Stan 1982
Gaydos, Kent 1969,70,71
Giardino, Wayne 1964,65,66
Gibbs, Eric 1990,91,92
Gibbs, Shane 1970,71,72
Gilbert, James 1978,79,80,81
Gildea, Steve 1968,69,70
Gilman, Brent 1968,69
Gilmer, Steve 1991,92
Glass, Chip 1966,67,68
Glass, Mike 1970,71,72
Glenn, Billy 1992
Glisson, Guy 1969,70,71
Glosson, Doug 1973
Goldsmith, Joe 1972,73,74
Good, Mike 1976,77,78,79
Graganella, Jim 1983
Graham, Jerry 1956,57,58
Grant, Kevin 1986,87,89
Gray, Darryl 1982,84,85
Gray, Hector 1978,79
Gray, Mike 1968
Green, Danny 1971,72,73
Green, Larry 1965,66,67
Gridley, Buddy 1969,70,71
Griffin, Chris 1973,74,75
Griffis, Kevin 1983
Griggley, Terry 1984
Grimes, Fred 1959,60,61
Guerrier, Dulack 1992
Gunter, Bill 1967,68
Gunter, Cliff 1961,62,64
Gurr, Doug 1966,67,68
Guthrie, Grant 1967,68,69
Hadley, John 1985,86,87,88
Haggins, Odell 1986,87,88,89
Hall, Chris 1989,92
Hall, Phillip 1982,83
Hall, Randy 1968,69
Hammond, Kim 1966,67
Hanks, David 1977
Hanna, Warren 1981,82
Hardy, Jack 1958,59,60
Harllee, John 1961,62
Harlow, Brian 1982
Harmeling, John 1973,76
Harp, Herbert 1982,83
Harp, Thomas 1986,87
Harris, Felix 1990,91,92
Harris, James 1979,80,81
Harris, Larry 1980,81,82
Harris, Wes 1986
Harrison, Bruce 1974,75,76
Hart, Ken 1966,67,68

Hart, Warren 1990,91
Hayes, Eric 1986,87,88,89
Hayes, Felton 1985,86,87,88
Haynes, Hayward 1988,89,90
Heath, Mike 1992
Hebron, Tim 1985,86
Heggie, Bruce 1983,84,85,86
Heggins, Jimmy 1974,75,76,77
Henderson, Nat 1977,78
Hendley, Jim 1984,85,86
Henry, Ferrell 1961,62,63
Henry, Gary 1978,79,80,82
Henry, Tommy 1990,91,92
Henson, Bill 1970,71
Hermann, Dick 1962,63,64
Hernandez, Jesus 1992
Herring, Reggie 1978,79,80
Hester, Jessie 1981,82,83,84
Hester, Ron 1980,81
Hiatt, Phil 1968
Hillabrand, Tom 1960,61,62
Hinson, Ron 1959
Holloman, Darrin 1984,85,86
Holloman, Tanner 1985,86
Holmes, Scott 1992
Holton, Steve 1957,58
Hood, Larry 1960,61
Hooks, Jim 1957,58,59
Horner, Alonzo 1992
Hosack, John 1965,66
Houpe, Gene 1988,89,90
Houston, Rick 1980
Howell, Bobby 1970
Huff, Gary 1970,71,72
Hughes, Bill 1968
Humes, Earl 1973,74
Hunt, Charlie 1970,71,72
Hunter, Ivory Joe 1977,78,79
Hurst, John 1966
Ionata, John 1982,83,84,85
Ionata, Joe 1986
Jackson, Bobby 1974,75,76,77
Jackson, Lenx 1983
Jackson, Sean 1990,91,92
Jacobi, Howard 1971,72
Jacobs, Greg 1984
James, Corey 1990,92
Jarrett, James 1969,70,71
Jax, Garth 1982,83,84,85
Johnson, Brad 1988,89,90,91
Johnson, Greg 1973,74,75
Johnson, Hardis 1979,80
Johnson, Homes 1979
Johnson, Lonnie 1990,91,92
Johnson, Reggie 1987,88,89,90
Johnson, Tony 1981,82,83
Johnson, Wade 1974,76,77
Johnson, Wayne 1967,68,69
Johnston, Duke 1967,68,69
Jones, Bob 1972,73,74
Jones, Cedric 1981,82,83,84
Jones, Cletis 1983,84,85
Jones, Donovan 1967
Jones, Fred 1983,84,85,86
Jones, Hassan 1982,83,84,85
Jones, Jerry 1965,66,67
Jones, Keith 1978,79,80
Jones, Keith 1990
Jones, Larry 1973
Jones, Marvin 1990,91,92
Jones, Phil 1973,74,75
Jones, Willie 1975,76,77,78
Jordan, Jimmy 1976,77,78,79
Kaiser, Randy 1973,74
Kanell, Danny 1992
Keen, Chris 1990,91
Kestner, Ken 1968,69,70
Key, Larry 1974,75,76,77
Keyes, Robert 1976
Kimber, Bill 1957,58
Kincaid, Mike 1975,76,77,78
Kinderman, Keith 1961,62
King, Grady 1978,79,80
King, Phillip 1990
Kinnaman, Joe 1966,67
Kinnan, Joe 1966,67
Kinsey, Rocky 1982,83,84
Kissam, Larry 1965,66
Kissner, Mike 1974,75,76
Klesius, Steve 1959,60,61

Knight, Mack 1990,91
Knox, Kevin 1990,91,92
Kolbus, Marty 1966
Kuipers, Jason 1986,87,88
Lamb, Ray 1958,59,60
Lanahan, John 1969,70,71
Lanier, Ken 1977,78,79,80
LeSane, Bruce 1987,88,89
Laureano, Juan 1992
Lazzaro, Greg 1976,77
Lee, Amp 1989,90,91
Leggett, Jeff 1974,75,76
Levings, John 1960,61,62
Lewis, Buzzy 1971,72,73
Lewis, Ronald 1986,87,88,89
Loftin, Jim 1962
Logan, Randy 1968,69
Lohse, Bill 1968,69,70
Loner, Frank 1966,67,68
Lopez, Pablo 1984,85
Loucks, Garry 1972
Lowe, Ron 1969
Lowrey, Kelly 1981,82,83
Luallen, Eric 1989
Lundstrom, Brad 1989,90
Lurie, Howard 1964,65
Lyles, Mark 1976,77,78,79
McConnaughhay, John 1960,61,62
McCormick, Gene 1958,59
McCormick, Tom 1981,82,83
McCorvey, Errol 1989,90,91
McCorvey, Kez 1991,92
McCoy, Jerome 1984
McCrary, Brian 1982,83,84
McCullers, Dale 1966,67,68
McDougal, Tom 1973
McDowell, Bill 1963,64,65
McDowell, Gene 1960,61,62
McDuffie, Wayne 1965,66,67,68
McEachern, Robert 1968,69,70
McGee, Joe 1957,58
McGill, Eric 1990,91,92
McGowan, Mike 1972
McGowan, Paul 1984,85,86,87
McIntosh, Toddrick 1990,91,92
McKinnie, J.W. 1969,70,71
McKinnon, Bobby 1973,74,75
McKinnon, Dennis 1980,81,82
McLaren, Scottie 1990
McLean, John 1980,81,82,83
McLean, Richard 1964,66,67
McLean, Scott 1979,80,81
McManus, Danny 1985,86,87
McMillan, Eddie 1970,71,72,73
McMillon, Tiger 1991,92
McNease, Y.C. 1961,62
McNeil, Patrick 1991,92
McPhillips, Billy 1973,74,75,76
Macek, Mark 1977,78,79,80
Mack, Kim 1982,83,84
MacKenzie, Dale 1962,63,64
Madden, John 1978,79,80,81
Magalski, Paul 1969,70,71
Majors, Joe 1957,58,59
Malkiewicz, James 1972,73
Maloy, Rudy 1973,74,75,76
Mancini, Kevin 1988,89,90,91
Mangan, Bob 1964,65,66
Mankins, Jim 1965,66
Marion, Tyrant 1992
Mason, Bill 1988,89,90
Massey, Jim 1963,64,65
Mathieson, Steve 1974,75,76
Matt, Prince 1982,83
Matthews, Jay Mac 1965,66
Mayhew, Martin 1984,85,86,87
Menendez, Bob 1966,67
Merna, John 1988
Merson, Bob 1980,81,82
Merson, Scott 1982
Messeroll, Mark 1976,77
Messeroll, Scott 1973,74
Messer, Doug 1961,62,63
Meyer, Carl 1959,60
Miles, David 1971,72
Miller, Fred 1973,74,75
Milligan, Pat 1981,82,83
Mindlin, Jeremy 1978,79
Minor, Roger 1970,71
Mitchell, Doug 1969

Mitchell, Hodges 1972,73
Mobley, Orson 1982
Montgomery, George 1969
Montgomery, Hal 1966,67,68
Montgomery, Howell 1966,67,68
Montgomery, John 1969,70,71
Moore, Paul 1988,89,90,91
Moore, Ron 1958,59
Moore, Ron 1983
Moran, Terry 1958
Moreman, Bill 1965,66,67
Morris, Dan 1983,84
Morris, Mike 1988, 89,90,91
Mosley, Ted 1967,68
Moss, Anthony 1987,88,89,90
Mowatt, Zeke 1980,81,82
Mowrey, Dan 1991,92
Munroe, Art 1969,70
Murdock, Les 1963,64
Murphy, John 1972,73,74
Mustain, Don 1959
Nance, John 1990,92
Narramore, Lee 1964
Newell, Greg 1984,85,86,87
Nichols, Gerald 1982,83,84,85,86
Nicklaus, Steve 1983
Nelson, Lee 1974,75
Norris, Brent 1971
Oglesby, Paul 1972
O'Malley, Tom 1985,86,87,88
Oreair, Rick 1970,71,72
Orlando, Mark 1973
Ostaszewski, Henry 1988,89,90,91
Ostaszewski, Joe 1988,89,90,91
Overby, Roger 1974,75,77
Owens, Gerald 1992
Page, Mike 1967
Paige, Lee 1982
Pajcic, Gary 1966,67,68
Palermo, John 1972,73
Palmer, David 1984,85,86,87
Palmer, Sterling 1990,91,92
Panton, Pete 1983,84,85
Parker, Chris 1988,89
Parker, Clint 1970,71
Parks, John 1985,86
Parris, Gary 1970,71,72
Parrish, Joe 1963,64,65
Pasquale, Paul 1958
Passwaters, Earl 1972,73
Patterson, Jimm 1992
Pauldo, Willie 1990
Pederson, Don 1968,69,70
Peirce, Jason 1990,92
Pell, John 1968,69
Pendleton, Larry 1966,67,68
Pennie, Charles 1965,66
Pennie, Frank 1963,64,65
Petko, Joe 1963,64,65
Pickard, Fred 1958,59
Pickens, Chuck 1967
Pinckney, Maurice 1989,90
Pittman, John 1967,68
Pitts, David 1964
Piurowski, Paul 1977,78,79,80
Platt, Sam 1978,79,80
Player, Scott 1991
Pope, Edwin 1965,66
Ponder, David 1980,81,82,83
Porter, Dave 1974,75,76
Pounds, Greg 1972,73
Prescott, Billy 1976
Prestwood, Tom 1972
Prinzi, Vic 1954,55,56,58
Prior, Brad 1976
Pritchett, Ed 1963,64,65
Ragans, Bill 1987,88,89,90
Ragins, Smokey 1973,74,75
Rainey, Reese 1971
Ramsey, Greg 1977,78,79
Ratliff, Floyd 1967
Ratliff, Ron 1970,71,72,73
Rebol, Todd 1992
Render, Ricky 1981,82,83
Rendina, Mike 1981,82
Renn, Bobby 1956,57,58
Restivo, Sam 1981,82,83
Reynolds, Detroit 1973,74,75,76
Rhodes, Bill 1966,67,68
Rice, Barry 1968,69,70

Rice, Beryl 1968,69,70
Richardson, Bill 1985
Richardson, Ed 1977,78,79
Ridings, Jeff 1974,75,76
Riggs, Marty 1985,86,87
Riley, Eric 1981,83,84
Rimby, Bill 1969,70,71
Riopelle, Jerry 1983,84
Riser, Butch 1966
Risk, Alan 1975,76
Rivas, Vic 1974,75,76
Roberson, James 1991,92
Robertson, Ulysses 1983,84
Roberts, Dave 1987,88,89,90
Roberts, Gene 1961,62
Roberts, Marion 1961,62,63
Roberts, Oscar 1971,72
Roberts, Pete 1965,66,67
Robinson, Chuck 1961,62,63
Robinson, Terry 1985
Roe, Ken 1981,82,83
Rogers, Ramon 1958,59
Romeo, Tony 1958,59,60
Ross, Grady 1989,90
Ross, Keith 1985,86,87,88
Rushing, Tom 1975,76,77
Russom, Kenneth 1960,61,62
Rust, Benny 1969,70
Ryan, Eric 1980,81,82
Salva, Mark 1984,85,86,87
Sammons, Mike 1969,70
Sanders, Deion 1985,86,87,88
Sanders, Terry 1976,77,78,79
Sanders, Tracy 1985,86,87,88
Sanders, Troy 1989,90,91,92
Sawyer, Bill 1974,75,76
Sawyer, Corey 1992
Schilbrack, Scott 1988
Schmidt, Brian 1975,76,77,78
Schmidt, Derek 1984,85,86,87
Schrenker, Dave 1985,86
Schuchts, Bart 1986,87
Scott, Arthur 1977,78,79,80
Scott, Carlton 1984
Scott, Kendrick 1992
Scott, Stanley 1983,84,85
Sellers, Don 1960
Sellers, Ron 1966,67,68
Senior, Corey 1988
Sexton, Billy 1973
Shaw, Bill 1969,70,71,72
Sheppard, John 1956,57,58
Shinholser, Jack 1963,64,65
Shively, Randy 1972
Shiver, Clay 1992
Shiver, Stanley 1985,86,87,88
Shumann, Mike 1974,75,77
Simmons, Ron 1977,78,79,80
Simpson, Carl 1990,91,92
Sims, Jim 1960,61,62
Singletary, J. Keith 1975,76
Slay, Steve 1962
Slicker, Tom 1960,61,62
Smiley, Anthony 1983,84
Smith, Abe 1976,77
Smith, Barry 1970,71,72
Smith, Eric 1991,92
Smith, Kelvin 1987,88,89
Smith, Marquette 1991,92
Smith, Mike 1978,79,80
Smith, Sammie 1986,87,88
Smith, Tony 1982,83,84,85
Snell, David 1970,71,72
Snipes, Roosevelt 1983,84
Snyder, Dave 1961,62,63
Solomon, Jesse 1984,85
Southwood, Keith 1984,85
Sowers, Craig 1970
Sparkman, Don 1971,72,73
Spivey, John 1957,58,59
Spooner, Phil 1963,64,65
Stallworth, David 1989,90,91
Stark, Rohn 1978,79,80,81
Stephens, John 1964,65,66
Stevenson, Robert 1989,90,91,92
Stewart, Alan 1987,88,89
Stewart, Mike 1976,77
Stiehl, Eric 1984,85,86
Strickland, Larry 1970,71,72
Strickland, Oliver 1989

Strickler, Joe 1969,70,71
Stockton, Andy 1974,75
Stockstill, Rick 1979,80,81
Stokes, Jay 1969,70,71
Stroud, Todd 1983,84,85
Sudder, Rich 1992
Sumner, Avery 1963,63,64
Sumner, Walter 1966,67,68
Sutton, Lenny 1986
Swoszowski, Bob 1958,59,60
Sytsma, Henry 1962
Tanks, Michael 1986,87,88,89
Taylor, Henry 1981,82,83,84
Taylor, Rick 1983
Taylor, Thurston 1965,66,67
Tensi, Steve 1962,63,64
Terry, Nat 1976,77
Thames, Jon 1973,74,75,76
Thomas, Curtis 1985,86
Thomas, Danny 1968,69
Thomas, Eric 1983,84,85
Thomas, Gerry 1991
Thomas, James 1970,71,72
Thomas, Rudy 1974,75,76
Thompson, Jim 1982,83,84
Thompson, Shelton 1986,87,88,89
Thompson, Weegie 1981,82,83
Tillman, George 1960
Tomberlin, Pat 1985,86,87,88
Trancygier, Ed 1960,61
Turral, Eric 1990,91
Tuten, Rick 1986,87
Tyre, Bill 1961,62
Tyre, Lewis 1992
Tyson, Jim 1968,69,70
Ulmer, Al 1957,58,59
Unglaub, Kurt 1976,77,78,79
Urich, Bob 1964,65
Vanover, Tamarick 1992
Verbinski, Joe 1959,60,61
Vohun, Frank 1967,68,69
Voltipetti, Barry 1980,81
Wachtel, John 1961,62,63,64
Walker, Clyde 1975,76,77
Walker, Stan 1967,68,69
Wallace, Ron 1968,69,70
Wallace, Wade 1978,79
Waller, H.T. 1966
Ward, Charlie 1989,91,92
Warren, Scott 1976,77,78,79
Warren, Terry 1984,85,86,87
Warren, Tommy 1968,69,70
Weldon, Casey 1988,89,90,91
Wells, Chuck 1985
Wesley, Gil 1977,78,79
West, Tom 1963,63,64
Wessel, Joe 1982,83,84
Wetherell, T.K. 1965,66,67
Wettstein, Max 1963,64,65
Wheeler, Tom 1982,83
Whigham, Frank 1970,71
White, Gaylon 1984,85,86
White, Randy 1985,86,87
White, Tom 1969,70
Whitehead, Bud 1958,59,60
Whitehead, Willie 1960
Whitehurst, Dan 1970,71,72
Whiting, Mike 1978,79,80,81
Whittington, David 1988
Widner, Terry 1982,83
Williams, Alphonso 1985,86,87,88
Williams, Anthony 1986
Williams, Blair 1981,82
Williams, Brian 1981,82,83,84
Williams, Dayne 1986,87,88
Williams, Del 1964,65,66
Williams, Eric 1984,85,86,87,88
Williams, Isaac 1982,83,84,85
Williams, Phil 1978,79,80,81
Williams, Ricky 1979,80,81,82
Williams, Waldo 1975,76
Williamson, Larry 1965,66
Willis, Peter Tom 1986,88,89
Wilmot, Horace 1983
Wimberly, John 1990,92
Woodham, Wally 1977,78,79
Woolford, Gary 1975,76
Wooten, Jerry 1963
Wyche, John 1987,89,90
Xanders, Brian 1992

Bibliography

Brown, Ben. *Saint Bobby and the Barbarians.* New York: Doubleday, 1992.

Clarkson, Julian Derieux. *Let No Man Put Asunder.* Fort Myers, Florida: Julian D. Clarkson, 1968. [This is a history of the first ten years of the UF/FSU football rivalry.]

Cobb, Arthur. *Go Gators! Official History: University of Florida Football: 1889-1967.* Pensacola, Florida: Sunshine Publishing Co., 1967.

Coale, Phil. *FSU Football: An Inside Look.* Tallahassee: Tallahassee Democrat, Inc., 1992.

Jones, James P. *F.S.U. One Time! A History of Seminole Football.* Tallahassee, Florida: Sentry Press, 1973.

Kabat, Ric A. "Before the Seminoles: Football at Florida State College, 1902-1904." *The Florida Historical Quarterly.* July 1991, pp. 20-37.

McCallum, John D. *Southeastern Conference Football.* New York: Charles Scribner's Sons, 1990.

McEwen, Tom. *The Gators: A Story of Florida Football.* Huntsville, Alabama: Strode Publishers, 1974.

McGrotha, Bill. *Seminoles: The First Forty Years.* Tallahassee, FL: Tallahassee Democrat, 1987.

Miller, Jeff. *Sunshine Shootouts.* Atlanta, Georgia: Longstreet Press, 1992.

Proctor, Samuel and Wright Langley. *Gator History: A Pictorial History of the University of Florida.* Gainesville, FL: South Star Publ. Co., 1986.

Spurrier, Steve, with Norm Carlson. *Gators: The Inside Story of Florida's First SEC Title.* Orlando: Tribune Publishing, 1992.

Sugar, Bert Randolph, editor. *The SEC: A Pictorial History of Southeastern Conference Football.* Indianapolis: Bobbs-Merrill, 1979.

Wills, Martee and Joan Perry Morris. *Seminole History: A Pictorial History of Florida State University.* Jacksonville, FL: South Star Publ. Co., 1987.

Index